FACILITATION SKILLS:

The ASTD Trainer's Sourcebook

Books in The ASTD Trainer's Sourcebook Series

FACILITATION SKILLS:

The ASTD Trainer's Sourcebook

Dennis C. Kinlaw

McGraw-Hill

New York   San Francisco   Washington D.C.   Auckland   Bogotá
Caracas   Lisbon   London   Madrid   Mexico City   Milan
Montreal   New Delhi   San Juan   Singapore
Sydney   Tokyo   Toronto

Library of Congress Catalog Number: 96-76145

McGraw-Hill

A Division of The **McGraw-Hill** Companies

1 2 3 4 5 6 7 8 9 MAL/MAL 9 0 1 0 9 8 7 6

ISBN 0-07-053444-6

Sourcebook Team:

Co-Publishers:	Philip Ruppel, Training McGraw-Hill
	Nancy Olson, American Society for Training and Development
Acquisitions Editor:	Richard Narramore, Training McGraw-Hill
Editing Supervisor:	Paul R. Sobel, McGraw-Hill Professional Book Group
Production Supervisor:	Donald F. Schmidt, McGraw-Hill Professional Book Group
Series Advisor:	Richard L. Roe
Editing/Imagesetting:	Claire Condra Arias, Stacy Marquardt, Ellipsys International Publications, Inc., Kalista Johnston-Nash

Contents

Preface

I'd like to tell you how this series came about. As a long-time editor and resource person in the training and development field, I was frequently asked by trainers, facilitators, consultants, and instructors to provide them with training designs on a variety of topics. These customers wanted one-hour, half-day, and full-day programs on such topics as teambuilding, coaching, diversity, supervision, and sales. Along with the training designs, they required facilitator notes, participant handouts, flipchart ideas, games, activities, structured experiences, overhead transparencies, and instruments. But, that wasn't all. They wanted to be able to reproduce, customize, and adapt these materials to their particular needs—at no cost!

Later, as an independent editor, I shared these needs with Nancy Olson, the publisher at the American Society for Training and Development. Nancy mentioned that ASTD received many similar calls from facilitators who were looking for a basic library of reproducible training materials. Many of the classic training volumes, such as Newstrom and Scannell's *Games Trainers Play* provided a variety of useful activities. However, they lacked training designs, handouts, overheads, and instruments—and, most importantly, they tended to be organized by method rather than by topic. You can guess the rest of the story: Welcome to *The ASTD Trainer's Sourcebook*.

This sourcebook is part of an open-ended series that covers the training topics most often found in many organizations. Instead of locking you into a prescribed "workbook mentality," this source-book will free you from having to buy more workbooks each time you present training. This volume contains everything you need—background information on the topic, facilitator notes, training designs, participant handouts, activities, instruments, flipcharts, overheads, and resources—and it's all reproducible! We welcome you to adapt it to your particular needs. Please read the copyright limitations on page iv, then photocopy . . . edit . . . add your name . . . add your client's name. Please don't tell us . . . it isn't necessary! Enjoy.

Richard L. Roe
ASTD Sourcebook Series Advisor

Chapter One:

Introduction

Welcome to *FACILITATION SKILLS: The ASTD Trainer's Sourcebook*—your one-stop reference for facilitation training materials.

FACILITATION SKILLS:
THE ASTD TRAINER'S SOURCEBOOK

You can use this book in a variety of ways:

- The program designs may be presented with little or no modification.

- Trainers may use the learning activities and other materials to design their own programs.

- Trainers may use the materials to supplement the coaching skills training programs they are already delivering.

More and more the work of organizations is being accomplished by groups and teams. Team formation presents a striking example of how the shape of organizations is changing. Work done by teams is less and less a temporary arrangement and becoming more and more the permanent structure in organizations.

Teams are groups which have certain well-developed qualities like common values, common purpose, and high involvement. They are groups in which members have a strong sense of inclusion, commitment, loyalty, pride, and trust (Kinlaw, 1991). Throughout this book we use the term *team* to apply to any group of people who are joined together to accomplish work. These teams may be very highly developed and functioning as superior teams, or they may be groups which exhibit few, if any of the characteristics of superior teams (Kinlaw, 1991).

At the heart of every form of organizational change and improvement you will find teams occupying a dominant position. Teams are the primary strategy organizations use to empower their people and respond to the relentless demand to build customer satisfaction, improve work processes, and upgrade the performance of their suppliers (Kinlaw, 1991, 1992, 1995). The use of teams is the most obvious of all of the major strategies for making use of the mental resources of people, i.e., giving them the opportunity to demonstrate competent influence.

1

Teams provide a structure that eliminates the requirement for direct supervision. They provide a structure for delivering whole projects and for managing processes from end to end. They perform functions that only they can perform. Teams are the best way for:

- Integrating tasks.
- Integrating information.
- Maximizing competency.
- Managing performance.
- Managing uncertainty.
- Managing resources.
- Increasing enjoyment and reducing stress.
- Continuously improving quality.

The formation of teams and their successful development and use require a variety of supports and resources, e.g., management modeling of team practices and training in competencies like communication skills, effective team leadership, structured problem-solving skills training, and the like. In addition to these resources, however, there is one more which can play a critical role in the formation, development, and performance of teams. This resource is *skilled facilitation*.

The ever increasing use of teams has created a need for the competent facilitation of team meetings that is far greater than at any time in the past. This need presents a special challenge to HRD professionals to provide quality training for team facilitation. The need is, however, not only large, it has special characteristics. The kind of facilitator training that most organizations require is:

1. Training that not only focuses on training individuals to serve as team facilitators, but trainings which also help teams to manage their own facilitation.

2. Training that is lean and efficient and that is always focused on improving the performance of teams.

3. Training that is rigorous in its design and terminology so that there is never any doubt about what is being learned, why it is being learned, and when it has been learned.

4. Training that has a strong empirical basis and develops in people those competencies for facilitation which are known to improve team performance.

Everything in this sourcebook has been tested many times over in helping teams to conduct successful meetings and in teaching people how to facilitate successful team meetings. In writing this sourcebook we have returned to the root meaning of facilitate which is to *make easy or easier* (Kinlaw, 1993). Unless we make it easier for teams, when they meet, to succeed at their tasks, we have not facilitated their meetings.

The bias that we exhibit throughout this book is that the facilitation of meetings can only be judged by its results. Did it help the team spend its time in the most efficient way? Did it help the team make the very best use of its members? Did it help the team achieve superior outcomes?

How to Use This Sourcebook

This is a *sourcebook*. It is not a *cookbook*. It has been written with the assumption that the people who use it already have the basic tools for being trainers and have had some experience in delivering training programs.

Emphasis in this sourcebook has been placed upon giving trainers a conceptual basis for designing and delivering facilitation training programs. This emphasis means that trainers will find a large resource of learning activities, assessment tools, visual aids, and ways to ensure the transfer of learning. The trainer's notes provided with the designs in Chapters 4 through 7, on the other hand, are not transcripts of training programs. They define what materials are to be used at what time, how long each event in the program will probably take, give the trainer suggestions about what should be emphasized in introducing the various activities, and offer suggestions for making the transitions from one event to another.

This sourcebook can be used by experienced trainers in a variety of ways:

- They may use the program designs in the form that they are presented with little or no modification to these designs or the materials used in them.

- Trainers may use the learning activities and other materials to design their own programs.

- Trainers may use the materials in this sourcebook to supplement the facilitation training programs that they are already delivering.

Purposes of This Sourcebook

The general intent of this sourcebook is to provide trainers with a single, complete source for designing and delivering facilitation training which will:

- Equip people who have no previous facilitation training.

- Upgrade the skills of experienced facilitators.

- Equip individuals who will serve as the designated or permanent facilitators of team meetings.

- Equip intact teams who will take more and more responsibility to facilitate their own meetings and operate without an assigned facilitator.

- Introduce anyone who attends meetings to the knowledge and skills for improving meetings.

Training individuals to be facilitators is more common than training people in the skills of facilitation (who may or may not serve in the formal role of facilitator). Facilitator training usually assumes that one person will be the permanent or primary facilitator of the meetings of some team. Facilitation training, as described in this sourcebook, makes no such assumption. The training in this sourcebook can, of course, be used to train designated or permanent facilitators. But this training can also be used for the wider purposes described above.

Training whole teams to facilitate their own meetings is a particularly powerful way to use the materials in this sourcebook. This kind of training assumes that every member of a team can help facilitate meetings and that people who may serve in the designated role of facilitator and those who don't can benefit from facilitation training. Training individuals and training teams have value, and both kinds of training can be accomplished with the use of this sourcebook.

You will not find in the following pages a cookbook about facilitating team meetings. You will not find simple-minded recipes that you can follow by rote to cook up a successful facilitation training program. What you will find is material to help you understand fully what *superior* facilitation is and how to plan and conduct programs to train people to be superior facilitators.

The specific purposes of this sourcebook are to give you:

1. A clear and concrete understanding of *The Meaning of Superior Facilitation*.

2. A clear understanding of *The Model for Superior Facilitation* and how it is used as the basis for designing and delivering successful facilitation training programs.

3. Guidance for planning facilitation training programs and for preparing to deliver them.

4. Training modules and suggested designs for programs that run from one hour to two days.

5. All the exercises and visual aids that you need to design facilitation training programs.

6. Notes for conducting each of the facilitation training programs described.

7. Several assessment tools that you can use to enrich your facilitation training programs.

8. A list of references that you can use for additional resources.

Our expectation is that, if you use the information that we give you about facilitation and facilitation training, and if you follow the suggestions that we make for designing and delivering facilitation training, you will be successful as a trainer of facilitators. We also expect that, once you have begun to use the materials included in this sourcebook and deliver the programs that we propose, you will begin to create your own materials and discover for yourself many ways to make your facilitation training programs your very own.

Sourcebook Organization

This sourcebook has eleven chapters. These parts have been arranged to help you prepare to deliver facilitation training programs. As previously noted, we have deliberately chosen "facilitation training" rather than "facilitator training" in order to emphasize the idea that training people to facilitate a team meeting does not necessarily mean that we are training them for the full-time or part-time job of facilitator. This may, in fact, be the case. But anyone who wants to be a better team leader or a better team member can benefit from learning how to facilitate (make easy) the successful performance of the team. A brief description of each chapter of the sourcebook is found below.

1. **Introduction**

   This is the chapter which you are currently reading. In this chapter you are introduced to the purpose of this sourcebook and given information for finding your way into its materials and familiarizing yourself with the location of these materials. Additional topics that you will find in this Introduction are:

   - How to Use This Sourcebook

   - Navigating the Training Plans

   - Sourcebook Organization

   - The Meaning of *Team*

2. **Background**

   This chapter provides you with some essential background material that you require to understand facilitation and the conceptual framework for the program designs. This chapter helps you understand the meaning of facilitation, *The Model for Superior Facilitation,* and the six competencies identified in the model. The model provides you with a clear and graphic description of superior facilitation. It is this model which becomes the framework for designing and delivering the facilitation training programs described in Chapters 4 to 7.

3. **Workshop Preparation**

   Chapter Three gives general tips on workshop preparation, including how to design, administer, facilitate, and follow-up on the training program.

4. **One-Hour Facilitation Designs**

   Facilitation training, at its best, is a *skills* training program. It is recognized, however, that trainers may have a need to deliver quite brief programs about facilitation. These brief programs may serve several purposes, e.g., introduce the subject of facilitation, provide an overview of facilitation training, reinforce some specific idea that people may have already been exposed to, and extend learning begun in earlier training sessions. This chapter provides guidance and examples for delivering one-hour facilitation programs.

5. Half-Day Facilitation Design

It is possible to conduct facilitation training over an extended period of time and divide the training into one-day or half-day training sessions. The two-day design described in Chapter 7 can, for example, be broken down into a series of smaller training sessions, i.e., one-day and half-day programs. Also, it is possible that trainers may only want to give people an extended introduction to facilitation. A half-day program can serve that purpose. In addition, half-day programs can be used to reinforce previous learning and give participants additional skill practice in some aspect of facilitation not covered in previous programs. This chapter contains an example of a half-day program and guidance for delivering the program.

6. One-Day Facilitation Design

This chapter of the sourcebook describes in detail everything the trainer needs to deliver a one-day facilitation training program. A one-day design can be a self-contained program that makes no assumptions about previous programs or programs to follow. It is, of course, as suggested in the case of the half-day program, possible to use one-day programs to deliver the more ambitious two-day program just by breaking this longer program into one-day sessions that might be offered over a period of time.

7. Two-Day Facilitation Design

The two-day design permits participants to do a great deal more than just learn about facilitation and *The Model for Superior Facilitation*. They are involved in a number of skill-building exercises, and on day two participate in videotaped practice interactions. The two-day design provides a good foundation in facilitation skills and participants can be offered additional training at some later date.

8. Learning Activities

There are three sections to this chapter: exercises, learning transfer tools, and program evaluation forms. All the exercises included in this chapter require participation and interaction. The most powerful tool that we now have for teaching new communication behaviors to people is video. We have included a number of exercises that make extensive use of videotaping and feedback. There are more exercises included in this chapter than are actually used in any of the program designs described in Chapters 4, 5, 6, and 7. These additional exercises provide trainers with a resource for designing their own programs and for offering their clients a variety of programs that can follow the use of any of the designs in this sourcebook. In this chapter you will also find a number of ways to help ensure that participants transfer and apply the facilitation skills gained in your programs.

9. Using the Assessment Tools

A very useful learning method in any training program is to help participants assess their own understanding and competencies related to the subject being covered. You will find in this section several assessment tools that you may incorporate into your facilitation training programs.

10. Using the Rational Tools

This chapter contains a description of rational tools in three categories: developing information and ideas, making decisions and evaluating alternatives, and quality improvement. Learning to use rational tools is one of the competencies required for the superior facilitation of team meetings.

11. Visual Aids

This chapter includes all of the overheads that you require to conduct your programs. These overheads can, of course, be made into other kinds of visual aids like flipcharts or slides. The materials in this section support all the presentations that trainers may make during a facilitation training program. In addition, they can be used as handouts or included as content in participant notebooks.

Appendix: Recommended Resources

The appendix contains a list of references and resources which have been briefly annotated to assist trainers in selecting the ones that might be most relevant to their needs.

Workshop Building Blocks

In this sourcebook, you have all the building blocks needed to create your own facilitation training programs. The following pages provide Subject/Reference matrices to help you select the building blocks that fit your objectives.

Directions

To choose the building blocks needed for your training program, follow the steps below:

1. To locate sourcebook material on a specific topic, go to Column A and find the row that lists the topic needed.

2. Refer to the cells in that row to find page references for information and materials on the topic.

Subject/Reference Matrix

A. Topic	B. Information	C. Program Scripts	D. Activities	E. Trainer's Notes	F. Visual Aids
1. Trainer Preparation and Planning	• Chapter 1 • Chapter 2 • Chapter 3	• Chapter 4 • Chapter 5 • Chapter 6 • Chapter 7	• Chapter 8 • Chapter 9 • Chapter 10	• Chapter 8	• All overheads are in Chapter 11
2. Program Introductions and Overviews	• Chapter 2	• Chapter 4 • Chapter 5 • Chapter 6 • Chapter 7			• Welcome to the Model for Superior Facilitation (p. 265) • Welcome to the Model for Successful Meetings (p. 266) • Objectives for One-Hour Program: The Model for Superior Facilitation (p. 267) • Objectives for One-Hour Program: The Model for Successful Meetings (p. 268) • Objectives for Half-Day Program: Introduction to Superior Facilitation (p. 269) • Objectives for One-Day Program (p. 270) • Objectives for Two-Day Program (p. 271) • Half-Day Program Flow (p. 272) • One-Day Program Flow (p. 273) • Two-Day Program Flow (p. 274) • Program Norms (p. 275)

Subject/Reference Matrix

A. Topic	B. Information	C. Program Scripts	D. Activities	E. Trainer's Notes	F. Visual Aids
3. **The Model for Superior Facilitation**	• Chapter 2	• Chapter 4 • Chapter 5 • Chapter 6 • Chapter 7	• Clarifying the Model for Superior Facilitation (p. 124)	• Clarifying the Model for Superior Facilitation (p. 123)	• The Model for Superior Facilitation (p. 276)
4. **The 1st Competency: Understanding and Using the Meaning of Superior Facilitation**	• Chapter 2	• Chapter 4 • Chapter 5 • Chapter 6 • Chapter 7	• Understanding the Meaning of Superior Facilitation (p. 126)	• Understanding the Meaning of Superior Facilitation (p. 125)	• The Meaning of Superior Facilitation (p. 277)

Subject/Reference Matrix

A. Topic	B. Information	C. Program Scripts	D. Activities	E. Trainer's Notes	F. Visual Aids
5. **The 2nd Competency: Understanding and Using the Model for Successful Meetings**	• Chapter 2	• Chapter 4 • Chapter 5 • Chapter 6 • Chapter 7	• Blocks to Successful Meetings (p. 128) • Clarifying the Model for Successful Meetings (p. 130) • Clarifying Potential and Structure (p. 132) • Clarifying Potential and Resources (p. 135) • Clarifying Performance and Quality Communication (p. 138) • Clarifying Performance and Understanding (p. 141) • Clarifying Performance and Rational Tools (p. 144) • Clarifying Results and Achievement of Goals and Improvement of Team Competencies (p. 148) • Practicing Facilitation, Helping the Team Develop Its Potential (p. 153) • Practicing Facilitation, Helping Teams Perform (Communication) (p. 159) • Practicing Facilitation, Helping Teams Perform (Developing Understanding) (p. 167) • Understanding and Using Team Evaluation and Feedback (p. 174) • Practicing Quality Communication (p. 178)	• Blocks to Successful Meetings (p. 127) • Clarifying the Model for Successful Meetings (p. 129) • Clarifying Potential and Structure (p. 131) • Clarifying Potential and Resources (p. 134) • Clarifying Performance and Quality Communication (p. 137) • Clarifying Performance and Understanding (p. 140) • Clarifying Performance and Rational Tools (p. 143) • Clarifying Results and Achievement of Goals and Improvement of Team Competencies (p. 146) • Practicing Facilitation, Helping the Team Develop Its Potential (p. 151) • Practicing Facilitation, Helping Teams Perform (Communication) (p. 157) • Practicing Facilitation, Helping Teams Perform (Developing Understanding) (p. 165) • Understanding and Using Team Evaluation and Feedback (p. 173) • Practicing Quality Communication (p. 177)	• The Model for Successful Meetings (p. 278) • Quality Communication (p. 279) • Developing Understanding (p. 280)

Subject/Reference Matrix

A. Topic	B. Information	C. Program Scripts	D. Activities	E. Trainer's Notes	F. Visual Aids
6. The 3rd Competency: Understanding and Using Team Evaluation and Feedback	• Chapter 2	• Chapter 6 • Chapter 7	• Understanding and Using Team Evaluation and Feedback (p. 174)	• Understanding and Using Team Evaluation and Feedback (p. 173)	
7. The 4th Competency: Understanding and Using Quality Communication	• Chapter 2	• Chapter 6 • Chapter 7	• Practicing Quality Communication (p. 178)	• Practicing Quality Communication (p. 177)	• Quality Communication (p. 279)
8. The 5th Competency: Understanding and Using the Special Functions	• Chapter 2	• Chapter 6 • Chapter 7	• Understanding and Practicing the Special Functions of Facilitation (p. 183)	• Understanding and Practicing the Special Functions of Facilitation (p. 182)	• Special Functions of Facilitation (p. 281)
9. The 6th Competency: Understanding and Using Rational Tools	• Chapter 2 • Chapter 10	• Chapter 6 • Chapter 7	• Understanding and Practicing Rational Tools (Developing Information and Ideas) (p. 194) • Understanding and Practicing Rational Tools (Making Decisions and Evaluation Alternatives) (p. 200) • Understanding and Practicing Rational Tools (Quality Improvement) (p. 206) • Chapter 10	• Understanding and Practicing Rational Tools (Developing Information and Ideas) (p. 192) • Understanding and Practicing Rational Tools (Making Decisions and Evaluation Alternatives) (p. 198) • Understanding and Practicing Rational Tools (Quality Improvement) (p. 204)	• Types of Rational Tools (p. 282) • Tools for Generating Information and Ideas (p. 283) • Tools for Making Decisions and Evaluating Alternatives (p. 284) • Tools for Quality Improvement (p. 285)
10. Review and Action Teams	• Chapter 2	• Chapter 6 • Chapter 7	•	•	• Review and Action Teams (p. 286)

Subject/Reference Matrix

A. Topic	B. Information	C. Program Scripts	D. Activities	E. Trainer's Notes	F. Visual Aids
11. Program Evaluation	• Chapter 7	• Chapter 4 • Chapter 5 • Chapter 6 • Chapter 7	• Program Evaluation: Short Form (p. 223) • Program Evaluation: Long Form (p. 224)	Program Evaluation Forms (p. 222)	
12. Assessment of Learning and Application	• Chapter 9		• Facilitation Analysis Questionnaire (FAQ): Self (p. 229) • FAQ: Other (p. 230) • Facilitator Competencies Assessment (FCA) (p. 232) • The Follow-Up Interview (p. 235) • Follow-Up Questionnaire (p. 237)	• Using the Facilitation Analysis Questionnaire (FAQ) (p. 228) • Using the Facilitation Competencies Assessments (FCA) (p. 231) • Using the Follow-Up Interview (p. 234) • Using the Follow-Up Questionnaire (p. 236) • Pre- and Post- Program Videotaping (p. 238)	

Navigating the Training Plans

The training plans are the heart of each of the seminar and workshop sessions. These training plans are set out in detail on a module-by-module basis, with an agenda, statement of purpose, and objectives for each module. We have attempted to make these training plans as easy to use and as complete as possible. The icons are translated on the next page and a sample page with annotations is on page 17.

1. Each section within a module has a heading that includes a statement of purpose for the section and suggested timing.

2. Within each section, you will find one or more major activities, each marked by an icon and a descriptive heading.

3. Additionally, you will find a number of supporting activities, each marked with an icon and explained with a suggested action.

4. Suggested actions are shown in conjunction with supporting activities, with the appropriate action verb in *UPPERCASE BOLD ITALIC*.

5. Suggested comments accompany many of the suggested actions. While these comments are fully "scripted," it is not intended that you "parrot" these remarks—but rather paraphrase the key thoughts in a way that is meaningful to you and the participants.

Understanding the Icons

Major activities

The following icons mark major activities:

Activities that feature facilitator commentary. In these activities, you—as facilitator—present information that will be key to subsequent workshop activities.

Activities carried out in table groups. You assign participants to small groups to complete the activity at hand.

Activities that revolve around total training group discussion. Such activities typically follow major exercises on which participants have worked individually or in groups. This icon is also used as a signal to listen for specific comments.

Supporting activities

The following icons mark supporting activities:

An overhead transparency is to be shown. The title of the overhead transparency is referenced in the text accompanying the icon.

A prepared video for interactive presentations is to be used with video-ready equipment.

A participant handout, part or all of a learning activity, or an assessment is to be handed out.

A question is to be asked. Wording for the question is provided, as are suggested answers when appropriate.

A flipchart is to be used. If the flipchart is one of the "prepared flipcharts" recommended for the workshop, its title will appear in the accompanying text.

Notes

The following icons mark notes to the facilitator:

Indicates a special note or suggested pre-work.

Indicates when to call time for timed exercises.

Marks the end of an exercise or section.

Sample Page

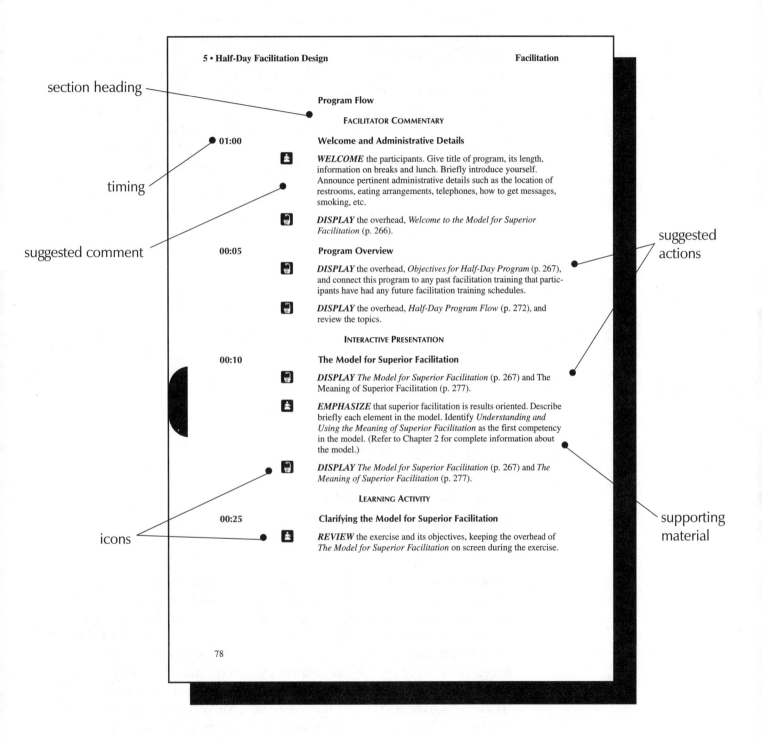

section heading

timing

suggested comment

icons

suggested actions

supporting material

The content of the sample page:

5 • Half-Day Facilitation Design   **Facilitation**

Program Flow

FACILITATOR COMMENTARY

01:00   **Welcome and Administrative Details**

WELCOME the participants. Give title of program, its length, information on breaks and lunch. Briefly introduce yourself. Announce pertinent administrative details such as the location of restrooms, eating arrangements, telephones, how to get messages, smoking, etc.

DISPLAY the overhead, *Welcome to the Model for Superior Facilitation* (p. 266).

00:05   **Program Overview**

DISPLAY the overhead, *Objectives for Half-Day Program* (p. 267), and connect this program to any past facilitation training that participants have had any future facilitation training schedules.

DISPLAY the overhead, *Half-Day Program Flow* (p. 272), and review the topics.

INTERACTIVE PRESENTATION

00:10   **The Model for Superior Facilitation**

DISPLAY The Model for Superior Facilitation (p. 267) and The Meaning of Superior Facilitation (p. 277).

EMPHASIZE that superior facilitation is results oriented. Describe briefly each element in the model. Identify *Understanding and Using the Meaning of Superior Facilitation* as the first competency in the model. (Refer to Chapter 2 for complete information about the model.)

DISPLAY The Model for Superior Facilitation (p. 267) and *The Meaning of Superior Facilitation* (p. 277).

LEARNING ACTIVITY

00:25   **Clarifying the Model for Superior Facilitation**

REVIEW the exercise and its objectives, keeping the overhead of *The Model for Superior Facilitation* on screen during the exercise.

78

The Meaning of *Team*

As already indicated, we use the term *team* to describe any group of people (i.e., two or more) who meet together to do work. Teams may exist in a multitude of sizes and anywhere within an organization. They also may take an unlimited number of shapes and differ along an indeterminate number of variables. They are short term or long term, created for a single meeting or are a permanent part of the organization's structure. They may have a simple purpose or a very complex one. They may have a single focus like improving some work process, or they may have a charter as broad as improving performance.

A few of the kinds of teams that exist in organizations are:

- Intact work groups.
- Subteams of work groups.
- Management teams.
- Action investigation teams.
- Design teams.
- Interface teams.
- Customer-supplier teams.
- Supplier-customer teams.
- Project teams.
- Advisory groups.
- Special improvement teams.
- Network teams.
- Committees and councils.

Whatever they are called and whatever their purpose, teams meet. When teams meet, there are opportunities for facilitating their performances.

In order to simplify the description of facilitation in this book, we use the term *team* to refer to every kind of team or work group that meets to do work and is small enough for everyone to participate fully in a meeting. A team may be a highly developed team or it may be a set of people who are meeting only a few times (perhaps even once) in order to accomplish some task. When *team* is used in this book, it should be taken in its most general sense to refer to any group or team that is meeting to do business. The team may be a well established team, or it may be a collection of people who have rarely or never met before to do business.

Now that you have a good idea about the contents of this book and how you can use it, you are ready to learn some more about the meaning of facilitation and how we will be using the term *superior facilitation* throughout this sourcebook. These are the subjects of the next chapter.

Chapter Two:

Background

This chapter of the sourcebook provides trainers with the conceptual foundation for using the facilitation training designs and materials included in the sourcebook. The logic is that trainers will make the most sense of the materials in the sourcebook if they know why the sourcebook has the shape it has and includes the materials that it does.

CHAPTER OVERVIEW

These are the sections you will find in this chapter :

- The Model for Superior Facilitatio n
- Overview of the Six Facilitator Competencies :
    - Understanding and Using the Meaning of Superior Facilitation
    - Understanding and Using the Model for Successful Meetings
    - Understanding and Using Team Evaluation and Feedback
    - Understanding and Using Quality Communicatio n
    - Understanding and Using the Special Functions for Facilitation
    - Understanding and Using Rational Tool s

The structure that underlies this sourcebook is the same that will underlie the facilitation training programs that trainers will deliver. This structure, or conceptual basis, rests on our definition of superior facilitation and the six sets of competencies that are characteristic of superior facilitation. Once trainers have the meaning of superior facilitation clearly in mind and understand the six competencies, they will see how the training designs and materials in this sourcebook fit into these six competencies.

The Model for Superior Facilitation

The meaning of facilitation used in this sourcebook is that it is a results-oriented activity. The position we take is that there is no facilitation unless there has been successful movement by a team toward the results for which it exists to achieve, and the team maintains or improves its competency for continuing to achieve results.

On the following page you will find *The Model for Superior Facilitation*. This model provides a graphic display of what facilitation is and the kinds of competencies facilitators must have to help a team reach its best results during a meeting.

The Six Facilitator Competencies

The superior facilitation of team meetings is not a random fulfillment of good intentions. Superior facilitation is *disciplined* facilitation. Facilitation requires that the person or persons doing the facilitation are able to make useful inputs into the interaction of a team, at appropriate times, to help the team move effectively and efficiently toward the goals that the team has set before itself. Being disciplined requires that facilitators master at least six sets of competencies. The six sets of competencies are:

1. Understanding and using the *Meaning of Superior Facilitation*.

2. Understanding and using *The Model for Successful Meetings*.

3. Understanding and using team evaluation and feedback.

4. Understanding and using quality communication.

5. Understanding and using the special functions of facilitation.

6. Understanding and using rational tools.

As the basis for facilitation training, the six competencies can be understood in this way. Participants first become familiar with *The Model for Superior Facilitation*. They then develop an understanding of the six competencies identified in the model. They practice these competencies and integrate them into a coherent and consistent process of facilitation.

The Model for Superior Facilitation

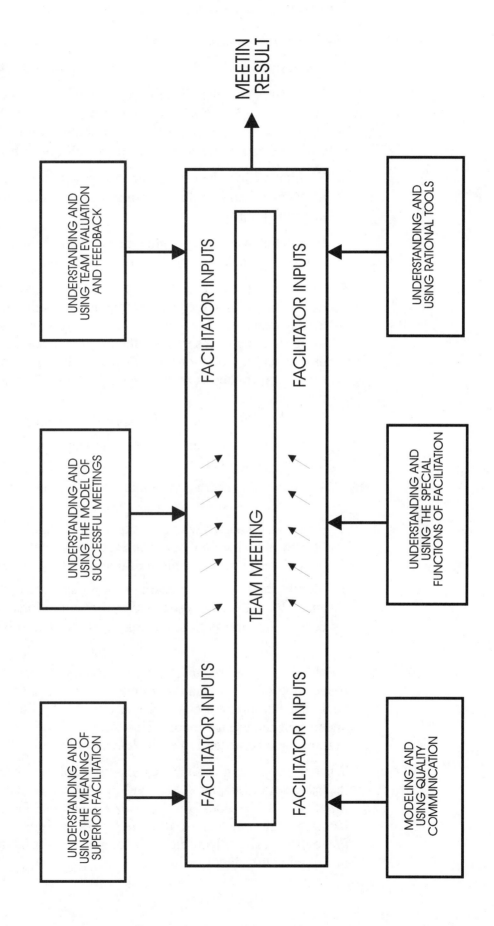

The Meaning of the Model for Superior Facilitation

The Model for Superior Facilitation is intended to convey:

1. The team is having a meeting to reach certain results.

2. Facilitators help the team manage the elements and subelements in *The Model for Successful Meetings*. Facilitators always use the model as their own reference for understanding what the team needs to do in order to achieve its best results.

3. Facilitators help the team achieve its goals using evaluation and feedback to monitor how meetings have been run and how they might be improved.

4. Facilitators use quality communication and help the team improve by modeling quality communication.

5. Facilitators perform, as circumstances require, special functions in addition to the primary function of facilitation (which is to help teams use *The Model for Successful Meetings*). This means helping teams manage their potential and performance or interaction. Situations may develop which require a facilitator to perform one or more special functions. These special functions are:

   – Be a *resource* and provide special information to the team.

   – Be a *teacher* when teams need to learn a new skill, like using a rational tool.

   – Serve as a *mediator* when individuals get at cross-purposes or become conflicted over an issue.

   – Be a *challenger* who may suggest that teams might try to go beyond what they have achieved and attempt a more difficult task or reach a more difficult goal.

6. Finally, facilitators help team meetings succeed by suggesting and helping the team use a wide variety of rational tools for developing information, making decisions, and solving problems.

The Model for Superior Facilitation provides the conceptual framework for the facilitation training described in this sourcebook. Facilitation training consists primarily of training people to understand and use the model. This means, of course, that they must become competent in each element of the model.

When trainers examine the programs in Chapters 4 through 7 and the exercises in Chapter 8, they will find the materials to be organized around *The Model for Superior Facilitation*. Participants in facilitation training learn to use *The Model for Superior Facilitation* by successively learning each competency for facilitation identified in the model.

Understanding and Using the Meaning of Superior Facilitation

We can assume that there are all kinds of meanings and definitions attached to the notion of facilitation and facilitator. Facilitation training can only make sense when we can describe what people are being trained to do. The more specific and rigorous we can make the definition of facilitation, the more specific and criteria-based we can make our facilitation training and the more definite our trainees can become about the job of facilitation.

Our interest is not just in facilitation, but in *superior* facilitation. There are three characteristics of superior facilitation which inform the process of facilitation and which determine how people can learn to be superior facilitators. First, superior facilitation is a results-oriented activity. There is no superior facilitation unless the team has been aided by a facilitator's input to more effectively and more efficiently reach its goals. Second, superior facilitation is a continuous improvement activity. There is no superior facilitation unless the team has been helped to maintain and improve its competency for achieving its goals. Third, superior facilitation is a disciplined activity. When we incorporate these ideas into a definition of superior facilitation, we obtain the following:

> Superior facilitation consists of inputs (actions) by one or more persons that help teams achieve their goals and maintain or improve their competencies to achieve their goals.

Notice again, that we have defined *superior* facilitation. We have selected this way of distinguishing the way facilitation is understood in this sourcebook from all other ways that facilitation is described. Facilitation, as used in this sourcebook, is always a results-oriented activity. When the inputs of facilitators are based on this definition of facilitation, we can expect facilitators to ensure that:

1. The first job of a facilitator is to help the team define clearly what it is trying to achieve.

2. Their inputs are focused on what the team is trying to achieve and not what the facilitator wants to achieve.

3. Their inputs are not just relevant to the present, but they have in mind helping the team grow in its capacity to perform.

4. They continue to enhance their own disciplined ability to facilitate.

Understanding and Using the Model for Successful Meetings

Facilitation, as used in this sourcebook, describes what one or more persons do during the meeting of teams that helps these teams proceed with efficiency and effectiveness toward their goals, while maintaining or improving their capacity to move toward these goals. Superior facilitation, therefore, requires an understanding of what a successful meeting looks like. What are the key elements in a successful meeting? *The Model for Successful Meetings*, shown on the following page, identifies these elements.

If you will refer to the model, you will notice that it suggests the following general ideas about successful meetings:

1. There are three primary elements that must be managed to ensure a team achieves its purposes. These are *potential*, *performance*, and *results*. These elements interact with each other and are affected by each other.

2. The *results* that a team produces are determined by:

   – The *potential* that the team has to produce the results.

   – The actual *performance* of the team as it interacts and tries to produce the results.

3. Each of the three elements has two or more subelements.

In the following pages we will look at each of the elements and subelements in *The Model for Successful Meetings* in detail. Also, you are encouraged to refer to the exercises in Chapter 8 of this sourcebook which further expand the meaning of the model. Trainers will find a full set of exercises devoted to teaching participants how to understand and use the model.

The Model for Successful Meetings

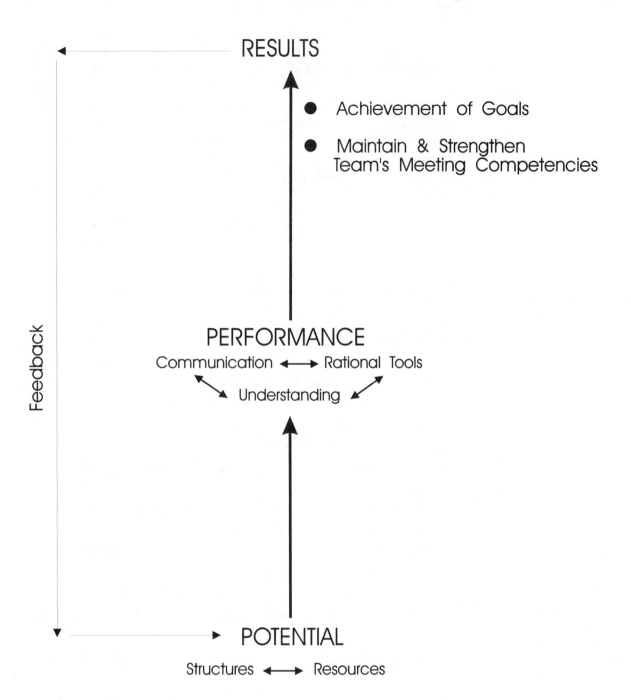

RESULTS

- Achievement of Goals

- Maintain & Strengthen
  Team's Meeting Competencies

PERFORMANCE

Communication ⟷ Rational Tools

Understanding

Feedback

POTENTIAL

Structures ⟷ Resources

Element #1: Potential

A meeting starts with a certain level of *potential*. This is the first element. A meeting may have a high or low potential for achieving success. The higher the potential, the more likely it is that a high level of success will be achieved. A team, for example, that is composed of people who do not have the knowledge or skill to perform an assigned task, has low potential. A team composed of people who do not know how to work together has a low potential. A team composed of people in competition with each other has a low potential. Teams which meet without having a clear purpose are also teams with low potential.

In general, the higher the potential that a meeting has to achieve results, the better will be the results. Meetings may not always achieve their potential, but it is certain that they cannot go beyond their potential. Facilitators help teams manage the potential of their meetings by helping them strengthen two subelements. These two subelements are *resources* and *structures*.

Resources

Resources refer to all the human, informational, environmental, technical, and material supports and means required for a team to do its best job during a meeting. Resources are strengthened by:

- Having the right people at a meeting, e.g., those with the necessary knowledge, skills, and experience.

- Having people at the meeting who are committed to the purposes of the meeting.

- Ensuring that people at the meeting have done their homework and are prepared for the meeting.

- Ensuring that relevant information is available to people attending the meeting.

- Ensuring that there is an adequate meeting room.

- Ensuring that equipment like projectors, flipcharts, and recorders are present—if they are needed.

- Ensuring that the time given for the meeting is appropriate to the tasks of the meeting.

- Ensuring members are skilled in team communication and problem solving.

This list does not, of course, cover all the kinds of resources that a team requires to do a good job at its meetings. The point being made is that the potential of a team to do a good job at a meeting must be managed *before* a meeting. One subelement that makes up potential is *resources*. Another subelement in the potential to have a successful meeting is *structure*.

Structure

It is not always easy to distinguish between resources and structure. Does making sure a team has a clear purpose increase its resources or clarify its structure? We could probably put such an item in either subelement. It is not so very important that we catalog accurately items as resources or structure. What is important is that facilitators think in terms of resources and structure, and recognize that these two subelements must be managed by teams to ensure that their meetings are successful.

Helping a team structure itself does not mean helping it become more formal. Remember we are talking about facilitating small teams to have the best possible meeting that they can, i.e., achieve the best possible results.

Structuring can be thought of as helping a team do whatever it must do to proceed in an efficient and effective manner toward its goals. When we help a team manage its structure, we are helping it take full advantage of its resources. Structuring means to help a team increase its potential to perform in a purposeful, rational, and fully conscious manner. When we facilitate the development of structure we are helping a team become explicit and conscious about such things as norms, roles, goals, and processes.

Norms

These are the rules and values that the team makes explicit about the way it will conduct its business during a meeting. Norms include such items as:

- Determining that a meeting will start and end on time.

- How each member will be assured of being heard.

- How conflict will be resolved.

- What is expected of each member.

Roles

Another way a team structures itself for a successful meeting is by making explicit what roles members will occupy and how people are expected to perform in these roles. Making information about roles explicit includes:

- Determining if a meeting will have a designated leader and what the job of the leader will be.

- Determining if there will be a facilitator and what the functions of the facilitator will be.

- Determining what other roles must be clarified, e.g., if the supervisor or manager of the team is present, how will he/she function during the meeting.

- Determining the goals of members representing special interests (e.g., supplier and customer, management and employees) and how these representatives will function during the meeting.

One critical step in facilitation, when there is a designated or permanent facilitator is that the facilitator ensure that his/her role is clear. Facilitators cannot assume that members present at a meeting have any experience using a facilitator or that everyone has the same expectations of what the facilitator will do.

Goals

Meetings are also structured by making explicit the goals or purposes of a meeting. Goals are of different kinds and exist at different levels of generality. A team, if it meets more than once, can be structured by:

- Making explicit the final or larger purpose of the team.

- Making explicit the purposes of each meeting.

- Identifying the specific products that will be produced, overall and at each meeting, e.g., reports, recommendations, data analysis, process improvements, and cost savings.

Processes

Meetings are structured not only by norms, roles, and goals, but they are also structured by the processes that are used. All meetings have processes. Processes are the sequences or patterns which teams use to carry out their tasks. They may use such processes intentionally or unintentionally. Teams follow a sequence or pattern, for example, when they discuss, analyze problems, resolve problems, or make decisions. Structuring the processes of a team means making a team aware of its processes or helping a team consciously select and use a process. It means helping a team begin to do things like:

- Decide (or at least make explicit) how decisions will be made. By the leader? By consensus? By voting?

- Make explicit who will take responsibility for decisions. The leader? The team?

- Decide if a minority opinion will be recorded with the team's decision.

- Make explicit what steps will be followed in solving problems and making decisions.

- Create and use an agenda.

- Make explicit the purposes or goals of each meeting.

- Select and use appropriate rational tools to develop information and solve problems, e.g., brainstorming, cause-and-effect diagrams, and the like.

- Decide if and how the team will evaluate its performance during a meeting.

Successful meetings are characterized, first of all, by teams which maximize their potential by ensuring that they have the necessary *resources* and have created the *structure* to permit them to perform at their highest level. It is, of course, the case that potential is not something that is created once and for all. It is being created and recreated over and over again before meetings occur and while meetings occur. Whenever teams strengthen their resources and improve their structure, they are improving their potential for their next meeting or the next event in any one meeting.

The second element in a successful meeting that is identified in *The Model for Successful Meetings* is *performance*. When a team actually begins to interact, it has begun to perform. Performance will, of course, be impacted by the team's potential. The higher the potential, the more likely it is that a team's performance will be high, i.e., its interaction will be purposeful, orderly, efficient, and the like. Performance, i.e., what teams actually do when they meet, is a function of how team members interact with each other, i.e., how they communicate, how well they develop and maintain the understanding of team members about what the team is doing, and how well team members use various rational tools to develop information and solve problems.

Element #2: Performance

How a team develops its potential to perform clearly affects how it is able to perform, i.e., carry on a meeting. But how a team carries on its business during a meeting is also influenced by how the team communicates, how well it develops understanding among its members about what it is doing or discussing, and how well it is able to use a variety of rational tools to help it develop information and solve problems.

Communication

The way a team performs during a meeting is a function of how it communicates. Communication that is most useful during a meeting is communication which has certain characteristics. It is:

- Interactive and Balanced

- Respectful

- Concrete

- Relevant

Interactive and balanced

Teams can use all of the resources represented in their members only when all members interact freely and when all members contribute to whatever a team is doing or discussing. Also, the interaction among members must be balanced. We have all had the experience during a meeting when one or two people did all of the talking. The purpose of a team meeting is to use the resources of all members. It is by all members asking questions, making comments, offering suggestions, sharing insights, providing data, and challenging each other's ideas that the team is able to do its best work. One task of superior facilitation is to help teams maintain communication that is interactive and balanced.

Respectful

Communication that works well is always respectful. This means that team members don't help the performance of their teams during a meeting if they ridicule or criticize each other, if they ignore the comments of each other, or if they minimize the value of any one's contribution. Being respectful doesn't mean that team members don't joke with each other or poke occasional fun at each other. But respectful communication can only be maintained when what each member says or does is accepted as potentially useful. A task for facilitators is to help team members practice communication that is respectful of each other.

Facilitators will recognize when a team isn't practicing respectful communication. It occurs when team members don't listen, when they interrupt each other, when they ignore each other's inputs, and do a number of other things which suggest that they are no longer valuing the contributions of other members.

Concrete

One way that teams become inefficient in the way that they communicate is that members will use language and ideas that are too general to be useful. What could it mean, for example, if a well meaning team member suggested that the team should "communicate better?" Such an idea might be useful, but until someone defines what particular ways the team is not communicating, the idea is too general. If a team member should define the characteristics of a difficult customer as "always wanting more than is reasonable," the team can do nothing to work the problem until someone has made the statement a lot more concrete. Another task for facilitators is to challenge vague inputs and encourage team members to be concrete in their inputs.

Relevant

A fourth characteristic of useful communication is that it is relevant. Being relevant means that an input is related to the work that the team is trying to perform. There are two levels at which work is done. The first is the *content level*, i.e., the information, opinions, ideas, or data given in the inputs of team members. The second level at which work is done is in the *process* by which information, opinions, ideas or data are developed and used. Process corresponds to any work process, like a production line, or the sequential steps for writing a technical paper. The product that the production line produces is analogous to the content of a team's interaction. How it produces its product is analogous to the process a team uses during an interaction. Processes may be quite informal, as is often the case as a team discusses a topic. Or processes may be quite formal, as when a team uses a rational tool like brainstorming. To be relevant, inputs by team members can either contribute to the team's content or help the team's process. There are an unlimited number of ways that team members can make inputs that are not relevant. Sometimes their inputs are "nitpicking," or "red herrings." They raise objections which are simply unimportant. Members also will sometimes make comments that relate to a topic or issue in the past or to something that the team plans to cover, but hasn't gotten to the topic or issue yet. Comments that are not relevant encourage teams to take unnecessary detours in their process, waste time on topics that contribute nothing, and generally contribute to the team's not proceeding in a logical and efficient way toward its goal.

Being relevant does not mean that team members should not be encouraged to contribute new or novel ideas. Ideas can be captured and tabled. They can be recorded and introduced at a more appropriate time during a team's meeting.

One task of superior facilitation is to help the quality of a team's communication by helping team members keep their communication interactive and balanced, concrete, respectful, and relevant.

This is accomplished in two ways:

1. The facilitator models quality communication in all his/her inputs.

2. The facilitator makes inputs which help the team improve its communication.

Developing Understanding

The Model for Successful Meetings suggests that performance has three subelements which interact with each other to produce the best possible interaction during a meeting. We have described the first two such subelements, using quality communication and using rational tools. The third subelement is *developing understanding*. Teams will move effectively and efficiently toward their goals to the degree to which members understand at all times what the team is doing and why it is doing what it is doing.

Understanding is created through the give and take of members interacting with each other. Understanding typically requires that

31

information be clarified or summarized. Understanding is also created by making connections and showing the relationships that exist among the information and ideas produced during a meeting. A major job of facilitators is to ensure that all members at a meeting understand what is going on at all times.

Facilitators help individuals understand in a variety of ways. The most frequently used inputs in superior facilitation which stimulate and support understanding are:

- Inputs That Clarify
- Inputs That Summarize
- Inputs That Make Connections

Inputs That Clarify

Inputs that *clarify* what is being communicated or clarify what the team is doing are inputs that stimulate and support understanding. One way to clarify what is being communicated is to rephrase inputs or request members to rephrase what they think another member has said. Another way is to help members become as concrete as possible in what they are communicating. Often this means something as simple as suggesting that members give examples of what they are saying.

Facilitative inputs that clarify are also ones that help keep the team conscious of what it is doing. These are inputs that remind the team what it has set out to do, letting the team know when it has gotten side tracked, or helping the team stick to the steps or rules of a rational tool being used.

Inputs That Summarize

A second kind of input that helps create understanding are inputs that *summarize* information developed by the team. Facilitators may themselves summarize for the team what has been communicated, or what has been decided, or what action is planned. Facilitators may also encourage team members to make their own summaries.

Inputs That Make Connections

A third kind of input that furthers understanding are inputs that help team members make connections. Inputs from facilitators that help a team make connections might sound like the following: "In the light of your deciding to do A, how will that affect your earlier decision to do B?" "Do any of the causes for the problem that you have identified share anything in common?" "Do any of these strategies seem to be at odds with each other—are they all fully compatible with each other?"

Rational Tools

A team's performance during a meeting is a function of the quality of the communication of members. Performance is also a function of the team's ability to select and use appropriate rational tools for developing information and solving problems. These tools structure the processes of interaction and communication.

Rational tools refer to any structured sequence of steps that help a team develop information or solve problems. A rational tool may establish the structure of an entire meeting or series of meetings by identifying each step that a team has set out to follow as it conducts its business. A rational tool may be as specific and finite as brainstorming, cause-and-effect diagrams, or the Nominal Group Technique. A rational tool may be as general as establishing the sequence for a discussion or the steps in solving a problem. For example, a team organized to improve a work process might organize a meeting or series of meetings around the use of a rational sequence like the following to develop its improvement initiatives:

1. Define the limits of the work process to be improved.

2. Identify and diagram all the steps and elements in the process.

3. Verify the steps and elements in the process.

4. Baseline the current performance of the process.

5. Identify opportunities for improvement.

6. Select initial opportunities.

7. Plan improvement initiatives.

8. Execute.

9. Monitor.

10. Revise.

During any one meeting this process improvement team might decide to use a specific rational tool. It might, for instance decide to determine if the process it is working on is currently under statistical control. The team will then select the appropriate statistical control model and make its calculations.

The facilitator's job is to help the team identify and use appropriate rational tools, to stay conscious of what they are doing as they use the tool, and to stick with the steps and procedures included in the tool.

Rational tools are, of course, closely related to structures. We have included them as a part of performance to emphasize that it is not just deciding to use a tool that is useful, but sticking to the steps or process defined in the tool that is required. Deciding to use a rational tool is the first step (structuring). Using the tool is the next step (performance).

In Chapter 8, trainers will find a set of exercises devoted to teaching participants in their facilitator training programs a number of rational tools.

Element #3: Results

The third and final element in *The Model for Successful Meetings* is *results*. Facilitation consists of inputs given by one or more persons that help teams maximize their potential and maximize the quality of their performance (i.e., their interaction and communication) so that they achieve the best possible results during a meeting. This definition suggests that there has been no facilitation unless the team has been helped to achieve its goals.

Meetings must be judged by the results they produce. A superior team meeting produces two kinds of results. The first result is that the team achieves its goals. It performs the tasks or completes the jobs that it set out to accomplish during one meeting or a series of meetings. The second result is that the team improves its competency for performing its tasks or doing its job. This second result is most clearly relevant to teams that meet more than one time. But individuals who participate in meetings with different teams can also be the means of improving the competency of all the teams with which they meet, provided they learn from each meeting how to improve their meetings.

Achievement of Goals

The immediate purpose of any meeting is to achieve a set of goals or perform a set of tasks. *The Model for Successful Meetings* clearly communicates the idea that the best results are achieved by managing the other elements and subelements in the model. Results are indirect outcomes. The degree to which teams manage their resources, structures, rational processes, communication, and understanding will determine the quality of the tasks they achieve.

Take the matter of clarity as an example. A team begins to manage clarity by properly managing the way it structures itself, i.e., the way it takes time to make certain the goals, roles, and processes of the team are explicit and understood by everyone. Clarity is also an issue in the performance of a team. Over and over again, facilitators will help teams clarify what they are doing and why they are doing it.

The kinds of tasks that a team sets out to achieve during a meeting is an open set. There is no limit to the kinds of tasks that teams have. Everything depends on the kind of team that is meeting. Learning teams will have their tasks, problem-solving teams will have different tasks, accident investigation teams will have still different tasks. Tasks obviously change with the nature of the team that is meeting. When work teams, process improvement teams, management teams, and other kinds of teams meet, they may have set for themselves the task of developing themselves as teams.

The job of facilitators is not to set the tasks for a team. The job of the facilitator is to help these teams clarify their tasks and achieve these tasks. Clarification starts with the way teams structure themselves and continues throughout their performance during their meetings.

Improvement of Team Competencies

A second result of successful team meetings is that members learn from each meeting so that they can improve their performance during future meetings. This result can, of course, only directly apply to teams that meet more than once. It can, however, apply indirectly as individuals learn from any meeting in which they participate so that they can improve any future meetings in which they participate.

The Model for Successful Meetings makes the improvement of meetings an explicit expected result. The model can be used as a tool for evaluating the way teams run their meetings and help them target opportunities for improvement.

Facilitation is accomplished by providing input to a meeting. One way for facilitators to determine when to input and what to input is by keeping in mind *The Model for Successful Meetings*. These inputs should typically address one or more problems related to the element and subelements in the model. When a facilitator is under the discipline of using the model, the facilitator will go through a sequence in reasoning like the following:

1. A problem or opportunity for improvement is observed, i.e., communication is confused, random, unfocused, etc.

2. The facilitator relates the problem to one or more of the key elements, i.e., asks the question, is this problem one of resources, structures, or communication.

3. The facilitator shares with the team what the facilitator has observed and is thinking.

4. The team, with the help of the facilitator, decides what should be done. For example, if the team has lost its focus, this may be because the goal or task is no longer clear, or it may be that the sequence of a rational tool is not being followed.

We have now looked at the second facilitator competency set, *Understanding the Model for Successful Meetings*. The third facilitator competency set is *Understanding and Using Team Evaluation and Feedback*.

Understanding and Using Team Evaluation and Feedback

We have now looked at the first two competencies required for superior facilitation. The third competency is *Understanding and Using Team Evaluation and Feedback.*

Three conditions must always be present for teams to improve their meetings. First, members must have decided by what criteria they can judge the success of their meetings. Second, they must decide how to assess their meetings, using these criteria. Third, they must actually assess and use the information they gain from their assessment.

Two tools which facilitators use to help teams assess and improve their meetings are:

- The norms that teams develop to guide their performance.

- The elements and subelements in *The Model for Successful Meetings*.

There are many ways that teams can use these two tools to assess and improve meetings. They can use video and occasionally tape their meetings to review their performance. They can use written feedback and anonymously complete a written evaluation sheet, if they choose. Data is collected and summarized by the facilitator, results are presented to the team by the facilitator, data is discussed, and opportunities and ways to improve identified. A less formal way is for the facilitator to present the criteria of evaluation and for the team to reach a consensus agreement of its performance on each criterion.

You will find in Chapter 8 exercises for training people how to help teams evaluate their performance and how to give feedback to teams to help them to improve.

Understanding and Using Quality Communication

When we reviewed *The Model for Successful Meetings*, we identified three primary elements that must be managed in a successful meeting: potential, performance, and results. In describing performance, we suggested that this was the actual interaction that takes place when people begin to conduct their business during a meeting. We further suggested that there were three subelements that account for superior interaction: using quality communication, using rational tools, and developing understanding.

Teams must learn to use quality communication to achieve maximum effectiveness and efficiency in their meetings. Facilitators help them achieve such communication by their own use of quality communication. Using quality communication is a major set of competencies required for superior facilitation.

We have already identified the key characteristics of quality communication as communication that is:

Interactive and Balanced   No one hogs the discussion and all team members participate fully.

Respectful   What is communicated does not target the mistakes, errors, weaknesses of members, but focuses on issues, problems, data, goals, and the like.

Concrete   Communication is concrete and easily understood.

Relevant   What is communicated is related directly to what the team is doing or how it is doing what it is doing (process or sequence).

Ability to listen   Underlying all quality communication and especially quality communication that facilitates a meeting, is the ability to listen. Listening is not an observable behavior. People can appear to be very attentive to what is being said, but in fact their heads "are out to lunch." We can only know that we are listening by the quality of our own communication. Facilitators can help themselves become good listeners by using the following tools:

1. We will typically hear and observe more if we maintain a physically attentive posture, i.e., look at people and don't distract ourselves by fidgeting or doodling.

2. Practice listening without evaluating or judging what is said; just concentrate on understanding what is said.

3. Practice reflecting back to the team what has been said, i.e., restate in your own words what you have heard.

Let us now look at each of the characteristics of quality communication in greater detail.

Interactive and Balanced

One task of superior facilitation is to help teams maintain communication that is *interactive* and *balanced*. This is the first characteristic of quality communication. Facilitators help team members maintain such communication when they model and use communication that is interactive and balanced. This means that facilitators never take over the conversation and always involve team members by asking them to verify what the facilitator says, by clarifying what the facilitator says, and by encouraging them to question what the facilitator says.

Respectful

Respectful inputs by facilitators are ones which have one or more of the following characteristics:

1. Are directed at issues, problems, content, and process.

2. Are not judgmental and convey an acceptance of any input made by persons during a meeting.

3. Actively help others develop their ideas.

4. Never block another person's attempts to develop an idea or contribute information.

5. Are never directed at the personal limitations or shortcomings of another person.

The way to understand respectful communication is to think about the kinds of communication that most of us have experienced in which we felt the communication conveyed a lack of respect for us. We typically feel a lack of respect by another person when we:

• Are not taken seriously.

• Are made fun of or ridiculed.

• Feel patronized.

• Have been interrupted or shouted down.

• Don't have a full opportunity to contribute our ideas.

Again, trainers will find a full development of the meaning of respect in the exercises devoted to quality communication in Chapter 8.

Concrete

Quality communication is always *concrete*. It is not very useful for a facilitator to advise a team that "it is bogging down," unless the facilitator is also able to say exactly what bogging down means. It is more useful to say something like, "you indicated at the beginning of the meeting that you wanted to explore other alternative solutions to the problem, but for the past ten minutes you have been discussing whether your management is really interested in any solution to the problem." It is even more concrete and more useful to say something like, "it seems to me that you have been stating and restating two opinions for the past half hour, without trying to look for any other alternative."

In helping members at a meeting decide on its specific purposes or goals, a facilitator can help the team by challenging them to decide what specific outputs they would like to achieve by the end of the meeting. For example, rather than settling for "discussing alternative computer networking strategies," a facilitator might challenge the team to list exactly what it wants to achieve by discussing such strategies, e.g., evaluating each alternative by a set of criteria like cost, ease of installation, hardware compatibility, and the like.

The first three characteristics of quality communication, i.e., the inputs made by superior facilitators, are that such communication is interactive and balanced, respectful, and concrete. A fourth characteristic of such communication is that it is always relevant.

Relevant

Relevant inputs are those which further the purposes of the team. We can, of course, never fully know before the fact if an input is relevant. We can only know after the fact because the input worked—it moved the meeting forward toward its goals. Input that is consistently relevant can be achieved as facilitators master all of the competencies identified in *The Model for Superior Facilitation*.

The major strategy for learning to make inputs that are consistently relevant is for facilitators to operate with a thorough understanding of *The Model for Superior Facilitation*. First of all, the model helps facilitators stay relevant by focusing them on the results that the team intends to achieve from a meeting. No superior facilitative input is ever random. Its intent must always be to move the meeting forward. Second, the model helps facilitators stay grounded in the full range of facilitator competencies, i.e., using all six of the competencies identified in *The Model for Superior Facilitation*.

Let us look at a specific example that illustrates how *The Model for Superior Facilitation* helps facilitator inputs stay relevant. The second competency identified in the model is *Understanding and Using the Model for Successful Meetings*. By understanding and using *The Model for Successful Meetings*, facilitators can analyze the behaviors of team members during a meeting. They can use the model to determine what kind of problem the team is having, i.e., is it a problem in resources, is it one in structure, or is it one in communication? It is only a matter of practice for facilitators to learn to recognize that a meeting isn't going very well because members present have not given enough attention to structure, or they are not interacting with quality communication, or that members have forgotten the team's norms.

Let us take another example of how understanding and using all the competencies in *The Model for Superior Facilitation* ensures relevant input by facilitators. The third competency, *Understanding and Using Quality Communication*. No input has a high probability of being relevant, i.e., moving a meeting forward, unless it has *all* the other characteristics of quality communication, i.e., is concrete, respectful, and process-centered.

Understanding and Using the Special Functions of Facilitation

Facilitators are always engaged in their primary function which is to help teams create the reality of the elements and subelements in *The Model for Successful Meetings*. In performing this primary function, facilitators help teams manage their *potential*, manage their *performance* or interaction, and manage their *results*, which largely occurs by helping teams manage their potential and their performance.

In addition to their primary function, facilitators may, on occasion, perform certain special functions. These are:

1. Be a *resource* and provide special information to the team.

2. Be a *teacher* when teams need to learn a new skill, like using a rational tool.

3. Serve as a *mediator* when individuals get at cross purposes or become conflicted over an issue.

4. Be a *challenger* who may suggest that teams might try to go beyond what they have achieved and attempt a more difficult task or reach a more difficult goal.

Be a Resource

A facilitator need not be an expert in the particular subject that may occupy a team. But a facilitator may very well be such an expert. Either way, there can occur times during a meeting in which a question of fact may arise. Questions like, "Who has that responsibility in the company?" "Is there data about this problem already available?" "Do we know of companies that are the best benchmarks for this process?" "What tools can we use to develop all the information we need?" When facilitators are asked such questions, their first response should be to put the question back to the team and find out if some of the members might be a resource. When members do not know answers to questions of fact and the facilitator does know the answer, then the facilitator takes on the special function of *resource*.

There is no reason at all why a facilitator should not serve as resource and help further the progress of a team during a meeting. It is patently dishonest and playing at the business of helping if facilitators "play a game" and act as though they cannot or should not be resources. The one condition that should always be observed, however, is that the facilitator never serves as a resource when members can be the resource.

Be a Teacher

The need to function as a teacher will arise most often in relation to helping team members learn a new skill to improve their ability to conduct meetings. When facilitators expect to work with teams over a period of time, one of the most useful things that facilitators can do is to introduce members to *The Model for Successful Meetings*. When members all work with a common understanding of the kind of meeting they are trying to create, they have begun the very powerful process of developing each member as a facilitator and helping the team assume responsibility for its own facilitation.

In addition to teaching members how to use *The Model for Successful Meetings*, facilitators can expect to teach members how to use various rational tools to develop information and solve problems. We will discuss the specific tools that facilitators should know how to use when we come to examine the fifth competency, *Understanding and Using Rational Tools*.

Be a Mediator

Strong disagreement and even conflict can develop among members of a team during a meeting. If the behaviors of members create blocks to the progress of a meeting toward its goals, facilitators can become mediators and help members resolve their differences.

If teams have included how disagreements and conflicts will be resolved in their norms as part of the process of structuring their meetings, the facilitator may have to do little more than remind members of their norms. If it is not possible to refer to norms, or if such reference doesn't work, the facilitator can proceed as follows:

1. Give the team the opportunity to decide whether it can proceed without resolving the conflict and come back to it later. Often conflicts at one point in a process become irrelevant as a meeting progresses. Also, members are often more able to resolve their differences at a later time. The conditions that created the conflict may have changed and the conflict or disagreement may have dissolved.

2. If the team feels the conflict must be resolved before the meeting can proceed, the facilitator can propose a process of win-win resolution. Your goals as a mediator are:

    •   Involve the whole team in the process of resolution, i.e., depersonalize the problem.

    •   Find a win-win solution to the disagreement or conflict.

Here is how to proceed once the team has committed to finding a solution to the disagreement:

1. Explain to the team how you intend to proceed. Put the steps shown below on chart paper. Ensure understanding and agreement.

2. Divide the team into two subgroups.

3. Have each subgroup take time to formulate as clearly and as concretely as possible a statement of the problem. Have each subgroup write an answer to the following:

   "What are the two positions? What does 'A' want or think? What does 'B' want or think?"

   The goal is to make sure that there is a problem, i.e., a real disagreement.

4. Have each subgroup put its statement of the two positions on chart paper. Facilitate a discussion of the statements. Give subgroups the opportunity to modify what they have written. You may find that there is no real disagreement, only a misunderstanding of the problem.

5. Next use brainstorming and develop a list of agreements between the two positions.

6. Now use brainstorming and develop a list of disagreements between the two positions. You may find now that the disagreements are trivial and that it is easy to reach a consensus.

7. If no agreement has been reached by this step, ask each subgroup to generate solutions that could satisfy people representing both positions. Have each subgroup place its solutions on chart paper.

8. Look for agreement or close agreement in the solutions. Select (as with every other step, by consensus) the most acceptable solution. You may find that solutions are combined and modified in this step.

9. Discuss the solution until it is stated in a form that "everyone can live with."

Be a Challenger

Teams never know what they can achieve until the members learn to work easily and well together. If you think of *The Model for Successful Meetings*, teams can always increase their potential for achieving superior results and can learn to perform or interact at higher and higher levels of efficiency and effectiveness. There can occur times, therefore, when it is useful for facilitators to help teams recognize their capacity to do more than they have done and to take on more and more challenging tasks and goals.

For example, if a team has been using an instrument to evaluate its performance on a regular basis and, over time, finds that it evaluates itself consistently very high, then the facilitator can suggest that the team look for more challenging ways to evaluate its performance. We remember working with one team some years ago that was using a five-point scale on several variables to evaluate its meetings. After a while, the team members began to rate their meetings as high as they could on all variables. When we suggested that the team might find a more challenging way to rate itself, it decided to use a ten-point scale to evaluate itself.

There are an unlimited number of ways that a team can improve its meetings. Teams can learn to use more and more kinds of rational tools. A process improvement team may, for example, start out by charting the steps in a process and then looking for opportunities to reduce the number of operations in the process, or eliminate waste and delay. Later, a facilitator might challenge the team to learn how to use statistical control charts to monitor and improve the process.

Understanding and Using Rational Tools

Facilitators must be competent in several basic rational tools for every aspect of solving problems and making improvements in performance. It is beyond the scope of this book to try and identify all of even most of the basic rational tools that a team can use. The growth of the total quality management movement and the many kinds of improvement teams that have accompanied the growth of the movement has placed more demanding requirements on facilitators to be competent in the use of more and more rational tools. What we have done in this sourcebook is to include a selection of rational tools that will have immediate utility for a new facilitator. Descriptions of the rational tools used in this book are found in Chapter 10. We have included tools in the following categories:

- Generating Information and Ideas

- Evaluating and Selecting Ideas and Strategies

- Quality Improvement Tools

All of these tools are supported by exercises in Chapter 8 of this sourcebook.

The tools for generating information and ideas that you will find described in Chapter 10 are:

- Brainstorming

- Nominal Group Technique

- Gallery Method

The tools for evaluating and selecting ideas and strategies are:

- Consensus Decision Making

- Plus-and-Minus Technique

- Priority Analysis

The tools for quality improvement that you will find described are:

- Flowcharting

- Cause-and-Effect Diagrams

- Pareto Charts

We have now looked at the six competencies for facilitating the meetings of teams. You have now been given the conceptual framework within which the facilitation exercises and programs in this sourcebook have been designed. In Chapters 4 to 7, we will describe the program modules and designs that you can use to plan and deliver your programs. In Chapter 8, we will give you all of the exercises that you will need to train your participants how to become superior facilitators.

Chapter Three:

Workshop Preparation

This sourcebook places emphasis on providing a conceptual basis for designing and delivering facilitation skills training programs. Trainers will find a large resource of learning activities, assessment tools, visual aids, and ways to ensure the transfer of learning.

The trainer's notes provided with the designs in Chapters 4 to 7 are not transcripts of training programs; rather, they define the materials to be used, how long each event in the program should take, and offer suggestions for making transitions from one event to another.

CHAPTER OVERVIEW

This chapter provides general tips on workshop preparation, including how to design, administer, facilitate, and follow-up on the training program. Topics covered include :

- Becoming Familiar with the Materials

- Trainer Preparation and Planning

- Facilities and Furniture

- Using Videotaped Feedback Exercises

Becoming Familiar with the Materials

Trainers will doubtlessly find their own way to plan and prepare to deliver a facilitation skills program using the materials in this sourcebook. We can only suggest to you, from our own experience, how to use this material to the greatest benefit. The parts of the book suggest this use. Here are the steps that we recommend:

1. Become thoroughly familiar with this sourcebook and its contents. If you have not already done so, you should read the complete sourcebook before you begin to plan your programs. As you do this, keep a notebook and record your questions and ideas for future use.

2. Once you are familiar with the sourcebook, read Chapter 2 to:

   • Develop your own clear rationale for facilitation.

   • Understand the definition given for superior facilitation.

   • Be able to describe in your own words *The Model for Superior Facilitation.*

   • Understand the six competencies for superior facilitation.

   You must become so familiar with *The Model for Superior Facilitation* and the six competencies that you are able to draw the model from memory and describe the competencies in your own words.   Each design and each exercise depends on the model and the competencies. It is essential that you are able to describe the model, the meaning of each of its elements, and the relationship among the elements. It is essential that you can illustrate each of the competencies with concrete examples.

3. Once you are completely familiar with *The Model for Superior Facilitation* and the six competencies, you are ready to understand the designs in Chapters 4 to 7 and the learning activities in the following sections. As you read the material, examine each learning activity as it is referenced. Make certain that you understand the objectives and content of each design, how they differ, and how learning activities, overheads, and other materials are integrated into the designs. By following this process, you will soon have a thorough knowledge of the material and know how all the chapters fit together.

   Although we have included descriptions of four different designs, trainers will quite likely modify our designs to meet the special training needs of their participants, to conform to the special constraints of their customers, and to capitalize on their own expertise and strengths. Making such modifications is quite easy, provided you have become thoroughly familiar with all materials in this sourcebook.

4. The next step is for you to read carefully through the entire set of learning activities in Chapter 8. Become clear about how each learning activity is structured. Pick out several learning activities and find where they are used in the designs. Become clear about the purposes of these learning activities and what outcomes you are trying to achieve with them.

Introduction to the Designs

The various facilitation training program designs are contained in Chapters 4 to 7. In order not to repeat general information which is typically applicable to all the designs, this section will introduce you to the designs and their common elements.

There are an unlimited number of ways that facilitation training programs can be designed. The length and content of a program will be determined by the following considerations:

1. How much total facilitation training do you intend to provide your target populations?

In Chapters 4 to 7, you will find designs ranging from one hour to two days. It is only the one and two-day designs which can deliver the results of demonstrated skill acquisition. It may be necessary, however, for a variety of reasons, for trainers to decide to deliver programs that will last less than a full day. Skill acquisition is obviously a function of practice, feedback, correction, and more practice. Programs that last less than two-days, unless they are programs that extend or reinforce previous learning, will not produce skill acquisition. They can, of course, produce various levels of cognitive learning.

2. Do you plan to use spaced training or continuous training?

Spaced training refers to training in which elements or seg-ments are separated in time. For example, a two-day facilitation program could be delivered in one-day segments or it could be delivered in several half-day segments. The half-day, one-day, and two-day designs that we have provided are presented with the assumption that they are complete programs. No assump-tion is made in these designs that there will be further facilita-tion training. There can, of course, be more training, but these designs give a complete description of what superior facilita-tion is. They differ in the amount of in-depth understanding of superior facilitation that is delivered and how much skill prac-tice is provided.

3. **How large a group will you train?**

The half-day, one-day, and two-day designs that we have provided assume that your training groups do not exceed eighteen
members. This provides three subgroups of six members each.
If you exceed this number, the designs that we have provided
must be modified. Each learning activity in the programs will
take more time to complete, the more participants there are.
The one-hour designs can be delivered to any number of people
because they are not skill development programs, but programs
to deliver information. If you are delivering information, then
any number of people can attend a program. If you are doing
any kind of skill training, whether new or to reinforce previous
learning, then the number of participants must be limited.

4. **Do you plan to use video to tape and replay the practice
    interaction exercises?**

Videotaping and replay offers the most powerful tool that we
have to improve interpersonal communication. We have, however, provided trainers with the alternative of not using video
and have designed interaction exercises for both video and no
video. If you use video, you lengthen the time that it takes to
complete a practice interaction exercise.

Program Elements

The half-day, one-day, and two-day designs all contain common
elements. The one-hour designs are special cases and will typically
contain only one or two training activities. The elements that are
common (with few exceptions) to the designs are:

*   Exercises.
*   Exercise debriefs.
*   Interactive presentations.
*   Transitions.
*   Reviews/previews.
*   Review and action (R & A) teams.
*   Learning transfer activities.
*   Program evaluations.

The meaning of these elements are as follows:

Exercises

The exercises in Chapter 8 are the foundation of all the programs
and have been designed to involve participants fully and to help
them assume responsibility for their own learning. The exercises
reinforce all the interactive presentations given by the trainer and
are the means for skill practice and skill acquisition. Full information about the exercises is found in Chapter 8: *Learning Activities*.

Exercise debriefs

The second kind of activity in the programs are exercise debriefs.

Debriefs give participants time to report the results of the exercises and give trainers the opportunity to sum up key learnings. Suggestions about what should be covered in debriefs are found with each of the designs.

Interactive presentations

All of the facilitation skills programs described in this sourcebook have been designed to involve participants fully in every aspect of these programs. The term *interactive presentation* is used throughout this book to describe a third kind of activity in the programs and to remind trainers to avoid purely didactic presentations and to ask participants to contribute their ideas and comments during every presentation made by the trainer. The exception, of course, may occur in one-hour programs given to very large groups.

Interaction is achieved by such trainer behaviors as:

- Asking participants to interpret the information presented.

- Asking participants to share their experiences regarding a topic or point made.

- Asking participants what they would do in such a situation.

- Encouraging participants to add information and ideas to the ones presented.

Suggestions about interactive presentations are provided with each design in Chapters 4 to 7. Visual aids to support interactive presentations are found in Chapter 11: *Visual Aids*.

Transitions

Another training element is the transition that trainers must make between activities in order to ensure that participants are fully conscious of what they are doing and why they are doing it. Suggestions for the points to cover in key transitions are included with the designs. Transitions serve the following purposes:

- Clarify the purpose of an activity.

- Connect one activity with what has gone before and what is happening next.

- Help participants know where they are at all times in the program's flow.

- Give the trainer the opportunity to summarize and reinforce key points.

Reviews/previews

Reviews/Previews are used in the program designs to alert trainers to opportunities to summarize key learning points at the end of complete units and to help participants anticipate the next units in the programs. The points to be covered in these trainer inputs are outlined with the designs in Chapters 4 to 7. The overheads and charts provided in Chapter 11 give trainers useful tools for making reviews and previews.

Review and action teams

In the two-day program, participants are organized into Review and Action Teams (R & A Teams). There is not time in any of the shorter programs to use R & A Teams, unless, of course, the one-day and half-day programs are follow-on programs and the R & A Teams were organized in previous programs.

R & A Teams meet during the programs in which they are used. Members meet at specified times with their teams to review their experience in the program, their key learning points, and discuss their personal action plans. They use their R&A Logs in sessions with their R & A Teams. Details about these teams and the R&A Logs are found in Chapter 8.

If participants are attending the program with people from their own organization, they are expected to meet on a periodic basics with their R & A Team to continue reinforcing their learning and to help members of the team continue to apply what they learn during the program.

During the time designated as a R & A Team activity, teams review their experiences and discuss how to apply their learning. For each R & A Team activity, trainers will give teams specific guidance for what they should accomplish.

Learning transfer tools

The obvious goals of all training conducted in and for organizations are three: (1) the most immediate goal is to transfer new knowledge and skills to the participants; (2) the second, and long term goal, is for participants to transfer their learning into their jobs and work environments and to make a difference in their own performance; (3) the third, and even longer term goal, is for this transfer of learning to improve the performance of the organization.

In the case of facilitation training, we should expect improvement to be produced in:

- The way individuals function as members of any team.

- The way team members assume more responsibility for facilitating their own meetings.

- The way designated facilitators assist the performance of teams when they meet.

The tools to help participants transfer their learning are found in Chapter 8: *Learning Activities*.

Program evaluation

The final element in all programs is program evaluation. In Chapter 8 you will find two forms. One is for use with the one-hour programs and the other for use with the longer programs.

Workshop Agenda Template

Use this generic workshop agenda template to block out your programs and plan what methods and media to use.

Agenda	Topics, Key Points	Time Allotted	Start	Stop	Training Method	Media	Sourcebook Pages
1. Welcome							
2. Overview							
3. Learning Activity							
4. Debrief							
5. Break							
6. Interactive Presentation							
7. Debrief							
8. Lunch							
9. Interactive Presentation							
10. Learning Activity							
11. Debrief							
12. Review							
13. Evaluations							
14. Adjourn							

Trainer Preparation and Planning

Detailed and specific information about each training design and its delivery is found in Chapters 4 through 7. All of these programs, though different in length and content, share a common requirement for trainer preparation and planning.

In addition to the questions about group size and using video (which we have already mentioned), there are other decisions that must be made in planning a facilitation training program. Decisions must be made about:

- Pre-program administration.

- Program logistic support.

Pre-Program Administration

Prior to attending a facilitation training program, participants should receive information about the program and what they must do to prepare for the program. They should receive at least the following:

 Send a program overview.
Send each participant a brief description of the program, including schedule, content, and benefits.

 State the location, date, and time of training.
Clearly state the date and time of the session and its location—and include a map to the training facility, if necessary.

 Provide guidelines for appropriate clothing.
Let participants know in advance if they are to wear business attire or casual dress.

 Provide a contact name and telephone number.
The name of a contact and telephone number that participants can use to obtain further information about the time the program starts and ends.

Program Logistic Support

A successful program will depend on trainers having taken care of the items listed on the next page. This checklist is provided to ensure that trainers leave as little to chance as possible.

Workshop Checklist

Program title: _____

Program date: _____ **Time:** _____

Name of facilitator: _____

Location: _____

Number of participants: _____

Materials Needed

Use the following checklist to make sure you have all the items needed for a successful program .

Training Setting and Facilities

☐ A meeting room large enough to accommodate participant teams.

☐ Separate tables for each team. All teams should have a clear view of overheads and charts presented by the trainer.

☐ A breakout room for each team, if needed.

☐ Tables for supplies.

☐ Extra seating for special guests or observers.

☐ Refreshment table (optional).

Materials and Supplies

☐ This sourcebook as a trainer's reference .

☐ Copies of all the participants' materials, one per person. It is a good idea to produce your own participant's workbooks from the materials in this book. There are handouts and, if you do not produce a workbook, then provide participants with a three-ring binder for filing and retaining program materials. Have a few extras of all materials just in case visitors or participants are added to the program at the last minute.

☐ Copies of Observation Sheets and interaction exercises.

☐ Copies of all the overheads to be used in the program, arranged in order of use .

☐ All charts to be used.

☐ Flipchart pads for the trainer and each team.

☐ Felt-tipped markers.

☐ Several rolls of masking tape .

☐ Name tents.

☐ Pens, pencils, and writing pads for participants.

Equipment

☐ Overhead projector.

☐ Flipchart stand for trainer and one for each team or table.

☐ Video-ready equipment.

Training Setting and Facilities

The meeting room should be large enough to accommodate all the participants attending the program. Remember participants will function as teams during the training program and should be arranged in teams at the outset of the program

Provide separate tables for each team. All teams should have a clear view of overheads and charts presented by the trainer. A break-out room is essential for each team.

In addition, there should be tables for supplies and seating provisions for any special guests or observers during the program.

Things to do   Prior to conducting the session, do the following:

 Prepare materials.

Before you present the workshop, photocopy the workshop agenda and script. Write your planned start/stop times and anecdotal material on the photocopy.

 Inquire about special needs.

Meet with the director of training and several of the individuals enrolled in the course to learn about any special needs, internal issues, and the experience level of participants.

 Develop relevant examples.

Develop examples that are relevant to the industry or enterprise.

 Encourage management participation.

Invite a middle or top manager to kick off the workshop and emphasize the important role played by supervisors.

Facilities and Furniture

Room setup depends on the group's size and room's physical characteristics. Possible configurations are:

1. Team Tables

The facilitation programs emphasize team participation—therefore, make sure the room setup provides sufficient tables and seating for each team.

2. Videotaping Exercises

For exercises which involve video-replay, provide seats directly in front of the camera for those serving as behavior models, with enough seating in the back for the rest of the team.

3. Breakout Rooms

Each breakout room should provide sufficient table seating for the team, with a flipchart within clear view of participants.

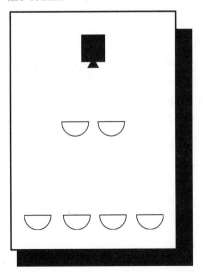

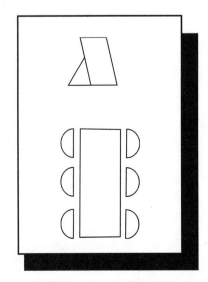

Audiovisual equipment

The facilitator's table, easels, and videocassette player should be positioned for clear viewing by all participants. The sound system should be adjusted so that everyone can hear videos, films, or words spoken into a microphone.

Power source

Find out where the climate control, light switches, electrical outlets, and sound system controls are. Also, obtain the name of the technician to call if you need assistance.

Supplies and refreshments

Place one table to the side for materials, supplies, and items such as a three-hole punch, stapler, and staple puller. If refreshments will be served, set those up on a second side table.

Facilities

Locate the phones, restrooms, vending machines, and cafeteria so that you can direct participants to them. Get names of nearby lunch spots if lunch is not provided.

Using Videotaped Feedback Exercises

There are several practice facilitation exercises which give participants an opportunity to test and apply the skills that they have learned. Videotaping and replay is strongly recommended for these exercises. Videotaping and replay is the best tool that we have for teaching communication skills to people. It is, therefore, the best tool we have for teaching the skills of superior facilitation. It is strongly recommended that trainers use the extended interaction exercises designed for videotaping and replay. You will find that the use of videotaping and replay is a powerful tool for ensuring that participants gain a sense of real insight and accomplishment.

Trainers are alerted to the following aspects of using a videotaping and replay format:

1. Video-replay provides participants with a great deal of information. It is important to keep them focused on the purpose of the exercises, which is for them to demonstrate their use of *The Model for Superior Facilitation* and the six key competencies.

2. Participants should stick to the use of the *Observation Sheets* provided with each of the interaction exercises. If not properly monitored, participants will give each other more feedback than can be used and get away from giving feedback that relates strictly to the skills and behaviors described on the *Observation Sheets*.

3. Feedback should emphasize the positive aspects of a participant's performance. At the very minimum, feedback must be balanced. Beware of giving participants too much negative feedback on their performance in the interaction exercises.

One way to enrich your training programs is to develop a set of video behavior models that illustrate the skills of superior facilitation. Behavior models are used to demonstrate to participants exactly what they will be expected to do when they facilitate team meetings. You can develop behavior models to demonstrate each of the six sets of competencies for superior facilitation. Use the models before participants practice each set of skills. Have participants use the same observation sheets for observing the behavior models that they use to observe and give feedback to each other in the exercises. There are several ways to develop models.

- **Collect examples.**

   The easiest way to develop a behavior model is to collect examples from the programs that you run. Most participants are quite willing to give you permission to use them as examples in later programs.

- **Develop behavior models.**

   Another way is to train a set of facilitators in an organization in facilitation skills and then have them develop behavior models. Use people of known positive reputation. This practice has obvious utility.

- **Assign a trained facilitator to demonstrate.**

   You do not need to develop a script when you make your video behavior models. Decide which skills you want to model. Assign a trained facilitator to demonstrate. Use a scenario that will be easily understood by participants who observe the model.

Name Tent

Superior Facilitation Workshop

Participant Name

Superior Facilitation Workshop

Participant Name

Participant Roster

Trainer(s): _____

Date: _____   **Time:** _____

Location: _____

_____

Participant Name	Extension	Department
1. _____	_____	_____
2. _____	_____	_____
3. _____	_____	_____
4. _____	_____	_____
5. _____	_____	_____
6. _____	_____	_____
7. _____	_____	_____
8. _____	_____	_____
9. _____	_____	_____
10. _____	_____	_____
11. _____	_____	_____
12. _____	_____	_____
13. _____	_____	_____
14. _____	_____	_____
15. _____	_____	_____
16. _____	_____	_____
17. _____	_____	_____
18. _____	_____	_____

Workshop Certificate

Certificate of Achievement

This certifies that, on

_____
(date)

_____
(name)

successfully completed the

Superior Facilitation Workshop

Congratulations!

_____
(Training Manager)

Chapter Four:

One-Hour Facilitation Designs

These one-hour facilitation program designs can serve at least the following purposes:

- As introductions to the subject of facilitation.

- As brief reinforcements of objectives or topics from previous programs.

- As a series of brief related presentations about facilitation that are given over a period of time to extend previous learning.

"THE MODEL FOR SUPERIOR FACILITATION"

This one-hour program has been designed to familiarize participants with *The Model for Superior Facilitation*, to ensure participants understand each of the elements in the model and how the elements of the model are related to each other.

"THE MODEL FOR SUCCESSFUL MEETINGS"

This one-hour program has been designed to help participants understand *The Model for Successful Meetings* and how the model is used as a tool for superior facilitation .

There are obviously a very large number of one-hour programs that trainers can give on facilitation. It will be extremely difficult, however, to build facilitation *skills* in one hour sessions—no matter how many of these you might conduct. Skill training requires:

- A clear understanding of the skill being learned.

- Time to practice the skill.

- Time to receive feedback on the performance of the skill.

- Time for more practice to benefit from the feedback.

One Hour Topics

In this section we will identify topics that are candidates for one-hour programs. In the following section we will give two examples of one-hour programs.

If a topic has been previously covered, then the one-hour program is used to reinforce an aspect of previous learning or to extend learning around a previous topic. If a topic has not been covered, then the one-hour program is used to introduce the topic. The point is that the topics may be the same, but they are being covered for different reasons.

We have listed the program topics below in two separate categories: introduction and reinforcement. All the topics listed under introduction can, however, be used as programs to reinforce previous learning as well as to introduce a new topic about facilitation.

Introductory Topics

Introductory topics that are used to acquaint participants with an aspect of superior facilitation will usually be general and cover a complete subtopic of the much larger topic of facilitation. One-hour programs used to reinforce previous learning or to build on a previous learning can be quite specific. Programs to introduce facilitation can be devoted to such topics as:

* *The Meaning and Importance of Facilitation*

* *The Model for Superior Facilitation*

* *The Model for Successful Meetings*

* *Understanding Team Evaluation and Feedback*

* *Understanding Quality Communication*

* *Understanding the Special Functions of Facilitation*

* *Introduction to Tools for Developing Information and Ideas*

* *Introduction to Tools for Making Decisions and Evaluating Alternatives*

* *Introduction to Tools for Improving Quality*

Topics to Reinforce or Extend Previous Learning

After a significant program in facilitation has been offered, such as the one- or two-day programs described in Chapters 6 and 7, one-hour programs can be used to reinforce certain aspects of the earlier training. All of the topics listed under *Introductory Topics* are, of course, candidates for brief reinforcement sessions.

Once a larger topic has been introduced, such as *The Model for Superior Facilitation,* one-hour sessions can be used to extend participants' learning about each of the remaining five competencies identified in the model:

1. *Using the Model for Successful Meetings*

2. *Using Team Evaluation and Feedback*

3. *Using Quality Communication*

4. *Using the Special Functions of Facilitation*

5. *Using Rational Tools*

To use another example, once the topic of rational tools has been introduced, later sessions can be held to equip people to use specific tools like the Nominal Group Technique, the Gallery Method, and Cause-and-Effect Diagrams. Chapter 10 has a description of a number of such tools.

One final note about one-hour programs. It will be difficult to use any of the interactive, videotaping and replay exercises to reinforce or teach any of the competencies of superior facilitation in a one-hour training program. The time required for these exercises depends on the number of participants in each exercise group. If you choose to use these exercises in a one-hour program, you will find that you must repeat these exercises more than once, to give all participants an opportunity to practice facilitating a team meeting.

Any of the topics that are introduced in a half-day, one-day, or two-day program can usually be turned into modules to fit a one-hour limitation. Trainers may find that it is useful to reinforce previous learning by having participants repeat an exercise.

In the following sections we have given trainers two examples of one-hour programs. These examples can be used as models for trainers to develop their own one-hour programs, using any of the introductory topics suggested. We have assumed in these examples that the program is a true training program and not a presentation of some kind. All of the topics can, of course, be adapted for use as presentations to conferences and other large groups. The two examples are: *The Model for Superior Facilitation* and *The Model for Successful Meetings.*

Materials Needed

These are the materials recommended for both one-hour facilitation designs. Page references indicate where masters for the materials are found elsewhere in this book. Unless otherwise noted:

- For overhead transparencies, you will need one transparency each.

- For other items, you will need one per participant, plus a few spares.

The Model for Superior Facilitation

Participant Handouts

☐ The Model for Superior Facilitation (p. 276)

☐ The Meaning of Superior Facilitation (p. 277)

☐ Clarifying the Model for Superior Facilitation (p. 124)

☐ Program Evaluation: Short Form (p. 223)

Overhead Transparencies

☐ Welcome to the Model for Superior Facilitation (p. 265)

☐ Objectives for One-Hour Program (p. 267)

☐ The Model for Superior Facilitation (p. 276)

☐ The Meaning of Superior Facilitation (p. 277)

The Model for Successful Meetings

Participant Handouts

☐ The Model for Superior Facilitation (p. 276)

☐ The Model for Successful Meetings (p. 278)

☐ Clarifying the Model for Successful Meetings (p. 130)

☐ Program Evaluation: Short Form (p. 223)

Overhead Transparencies

☐ Welcome to the Model for Successful Meetings (p. 266)

☐ Objectives for One-Hour Program: The Model for Successful Meetings (p. 268)

☐ The Model for Superior Facilitation (p. 276)

☐ The Model for Successful Meetings (p. 278)

1. The Model for Superior Facilitation

Objectives

This one-hour program has been designed to familiarize participants with the *Model for Superior Facilitation*, to ensure participants understand each of the elements in the model and how the elements of the model are related to each other.

Materials Needed

Participant Handouts

- *The Model for Superior Facilitation* (p. 276)

- *The Meaning of Superior Facilitation* (p. 277)

- *Clarifying the Model for Superior Facilitation* (p. 124)

- *Program Evaluation: Short Form* (p. 223)

Overhead Transparencies

- *Welcome to the Model for Superior Facilitation* (p. 265)

- *Objectives for One-Hour Program:*
  The Model For Superior Facilitation (p. 267)

- *The Model for Superior Facilitation* (p. 276)

- *The Meaning of Superior Facilitation* (p. 277)

Workshop Agenda

1. The Model for Superior Facilitation	Minutes 60	Start / Stop	Actual Start / Stop
Welcome and Administrative Details	05	8:00 / 8:05	_____ / _____
Program Overview	05	8:05 / 8:10	_____ / _____
Interactive Presentation: The Model for Superior Facilitation	10	8:10 / 8:20	_____ / _____
Clarifying the Model for Superior Facilitation	20	8:20 / 8:40	_____ / _____
Debrief	05	8:40 / 8:45	_____ / _____
Program Review and Wrap-Up	10	8:45 / 8:55	_____ / _____
Program Evaluation	05	8:55 / 9:00	_____ / _____

Program Flow

FACILITATOR COMMENTARY

00:05   **Welcome and Administrative Details**

WELCOME the participants and give the title of the program. Briefly introduce yourself (if you have not done so in previous programs with the same participants). Announce pertinent administrative details such as the location of restrooms, rule on smoking, etc.

DISPLAY the overhead, *Welcome to the Model for Superior Facilitation* (p. 265).

00:05   **Program Overview**

SHOW program objectives and connect this program to any past facilitation training that participants have had and any future facilitation training scheduled.

DISPLAY the overhead, *Objectives for One-Hour Program: The Model for Superior Facilitation* (p. 267).

INTERACTIVE PRESENTATION

00:10   **The Model for Superior Facilitation**

DISPLAY the overheads, *The Model for Superior Facilitation* (p. 276) and *The Meaning of Superior Facilitation* (p. 277).

EMPHASIZE that superior facilitation is results-oriented. Describe briefly each element in the model.

IDENTIFY *Understanding and Using the Meaning of Superior Facilitation* as the first competency in the model. (Refer to Chapter 2 for complete information about the model.)

DISPLAY the overheads, *The Model for Superior Facilitation* (p. 276) and *The Meaning of Superior Facilitation* (p. 277).

00:20   **Clarifying the Model for Superior Facilitation**

DISTRIBUTE the exercise, *Clarifying the Model for Superior Facilitation* (p. 124) and REVIEW its objectives, (keeping the overhead of *The Model for Superior Facilitation* on screen during the exercise).

ASSIGN breakout rooms, if used, and assign the time to complete the exercise and return to general session.

REMIND participants that they will be using the model in all future activities in the program (if there are such activities and programs planned).

GROUP ACTIVITY

00:05   **Debrief**

MAKE sure following ideas are brought out:

- Superior facilitation is any useful thing that any team member does or any designated facilitator does that helps a team have a successful meeting.

- Superior facilitation is based on the six competencies.

REVIEW each of the six competencies.

DISPLAY the overheads, *The Model for Superior Facilitation* (p. 276) and *The Meaning of Superior Facilitation* (p. 277).

00:10   **Program Review and Wrap-Up**

USE the handouts *The Model for Superior Facilitation* (p. 276) and *The Meaning of Superior Facilitation* (p. 277) to review and wrap-up.

DISPLAY the overhead, *Objectives for One-Hour Program: The Model for Superior Facilitation* (p. 267).

00:05   **Program Evaluation**

DISTRIBUTE copies of the *Program Evaluation: Short Form* (p. 223) to each participant.

2. The Model for Successful Meetings

Objectives

This one-hour program has been designed to help participants understand *The Model for Successful Meetings* and how the model is used as a tool for superior facilitation.

Materials Needed

Participant Handouts

- *The Model for Superior Facilitation* (p. 276)

- *The Model for Successful Meetings* (p. 278)

- *Clarifying the Model for Successful Meetings* (p. 130)

- *Program Evaluation: Short Form* (p. 223)

Overhead Transparencies

- *Welcome to the Model for Successful Meetings* (p. 266)

- *Objectives for One-Hour Program: The Model for Successful Meetings* (p. 268)

- *The Model for Superior Facilitation* (p. 276)

- *The Model for Successful Meetings* (p. 278)

Workshop Agenda

1. The Model for Successful Meetings	Minutes 60	Start / Stop	Actual Start / Stop
Welcome and Administrative Details	05	8:00 / 8:05	_____ / _____
Program Overview	05	8:05 / 8:10	_____ / _____
Interactive Presentation: The Model for Successful Meetings	10	8:10 / 8:20	_____ / _____
Clarifying the Model for Successful Meetings	20	8:20 / 8:40	_____ / _____
Debrief	10	8:40 / 8:50	_____ / _____
Program Review and Wrap-Up	05	8:50 / 8:55	_____ / _____
Program Evaluation	05	8:55 / 9:00	_____ / _____

Program Flow

FACILITATOR COMMENTARY

00:05   **Welcome and Administrative Details**

 WELCOME the participants. Give the title of program. Briefly introduce yourself (if you have not done so in previous programs with the same participants). Announce pertinent administrative details such as the location of restrooms, rule on smoking, etc.

 DISPLAY the overhead, *Welcome to the Model for Successful Meetings* (p. 266).

00:05   **Program Overview**

 SHOW program objectives and connect this program to any past facilitation training that participants have had and any future facilitation training scheduled.

 DISPLAY the overhead, *Objectives for One-Hour Program: The Model for Successful Meetings* (p. 268).

INTERACTIVE PRESENTATION

00:10   **The Model for Successful Meetings**

 REVIEW *The Model for Superior Facilitation* and show how using and understanding *The Model for Successful Meetings* is one of the competencies for superior facilitation. Review the elements in *The Model for Successful Meetings*.

 DISPLAY the overheads, *The Model for Superior Facilitation* (p. 276) and *The Model for Successful Meetings* (p. 278).

00:20   **Clarifying the Model for Successful Meetings**

 DISTRIBUTE the exercise, *Clarifying the Model for Successful Meetings* (p. 130) and **REVIEW** its objectives (keeping the overhead of *The Model for Successful Meetings* on screen during the exercise).

 ASSIGN breakout rooms, if used, and assign time to complete the exercise and return to general session.

 REMIND participants that understanding and using the model is the second of the six competencies used in superior facilitation.

GROUP ACTIVITY

00:10   **Debrief**

HAVE each team present its questions. Using a round-robin method, take a question from one table, a second question from the next table, and so on until all questions have been presented.

INVOLVE the whole group in answering as each question is presented.

REVIEW each of the elements and subelements in *The Model for Successful Meetings*.

DISPLAY the overhead, *The Model for Successful Meetings* (p. 278).

00:05   **Program Review and Wrap-Up**

USE the handouts *The Model for Superior Facilitation* (p. 276) and *The Model for Successful Meetings* (p. 278) to review and wrap-up.

DISPLAY the overhead *Objectives for One-Hour Program: The Model for Successful Meetings* (p. 268).

00:05   **Program Evaluation**

DISTRIBUTE copies of the *Program Evaluation: Short Form* (p. 223) to each participant.

Chapter Five:

Half-Day Facilitation Design

This chapter contains training designs for a half-day facilitation program—ready to go "as is" or to be tailored to meet your needs. The chapter is divided into five parts:

- Introduction

- Half-Day Topics

- Materials Needed

- Workshop Agenda

- Program Flow

"THE MODEL FOR SUPERIOR FACILITATION"

This half-day program has been designed to familiarize par-ticipants with *The Model for Superior Facilitation*, to ensure participants understand each of the elements in the model and how the elements of the model are related to each other.

The half-day facilitation program design can serve the same purposes as the one-hour designs. It can be used :

- An introduction to the subject of facilitation .

- As reinforcement for some objectives or topics of previous programs .

- As a series of related presentations about facilitation that is given over a period of time to extend previous learning.

Introduction

The half-day design provides time to accomplish a lot more than the one-hour designs. In addition, the longer one-day and two-day designs can all be delivered in a spaced training format of half-day sessions. Each of the longer programs can be separated at their mid-day points. It is not necessary, therefore, to provide additional information about these kinds of half-day programs. The information about half-day programs that follows assumes that these half-day programs are not half-day sessions of the one or two day programs. The assumption is that these half-day programs have the purpose of either introducing a facilitation topic, or of reinforcing or of extending previous learning.

As with the one-hour programs, there are a very large number of half-day programs that trainers can give on facilitation. The half-day programs differ from the one-hour programs in one important characteristic. Although it will be extremely difficult to build facilitation skills in one hour sessions, it is possible to do some skill training in the half-day sessions. This is especially the case where the half-day sessions are used to reinforce or extend previous skill acquisition.

Half-Day Topics

In this section we will identify topics that are candidates for half-day programs. In the following section we will give an example of a half-day program.

If a topic has been previously covered, then the half-day program is used to reinforce some aspect of previous learning, or to extend learning around some previous topic. If a topic has not been covered, then the half-day program is used to introduce the topic. As with the one-hour programs, the topics may be the same, they are just being covered for different reasons.

We have listed the program topics below in two separate categories: introductory topics and topics that reinforce or extend learning. All the introductory topics can, of course, be used as programs to reinforce previous learning as well as to introduce some new topic about facilitation.

Introductory Topics

Introductory topics that are used to acquaint participants with some aspect of superior facilitation will usually be general and cover some complete subtopic of the much larger topic of facilitation. On the other hand, half-day programs used to reinforce previous learning or to build on some previous learning can be quite specific. Programs to introduce facilitation can be devoted to such topics as:

- *Introduction to Superior Facilitation*

- *Understanding and Using the Model for Successful Meetings*

- *Understanding and Using Team Evaluation and Feedback*

- *Understanding and Using Quality Communication*

- *Understanding and Using the Special Functions of Facilitation*

Topics to Reinforce or Extend Previous Learning

After a significant program in facilitation has been offered, such as the half-day, one-day, or two-day programs, additional half-day programs can be used to reinforce certain aspects of the earlier training, or to build on previous learning. All of the topics listed under Introductory Topics are also candidates for sessions that reinforce or extend learning.

Once a larger topic has been introduced, such as *Understanding and Using the Model for Successful Meetings*, half-day sessions can be used for participants to practice using the model to facilitate a team meeting. Listed below are some topics that might also be used in reinforcement sessions, or in sessions to extend participants' learning in some aspect of facilitation.

- *Practicing Facilitation*
  - *Helping the Team Develop Its Potential*
  - *Helping Teams Perform*
    - *Focus on Communication*
    - *Focus on Developing Understanding*
- *Practicing Quality Communication*
- *Practicing the Special Functions of Facilitation*
- *Practicing Rational Tools*
  - *Developing Information and Ideas*
  - *Making Decisions and Evaluation Alternatives*
  - *Improving Quality*

Materials Needed

The following materials are recommended for the half-day facilitation design. Page references indicate where masters for the materials are found elsewhere in this book. Unless otherwise noted:

- For overhead transparencies, you will need one transparency each.

- For other items, you will need one per participant, plus a few spares.

Participant Handouts

☐ The Model for Superior Facilitation (p. 276)

☐ The Model for Successful Meetings (p. 278)

☐ Blocks to Successful Meetings (p. 128)

☐ Clarifying the Model for Superior Facilitation (p. 124)

☐ Understanding the Meaning of Superior Facilitation (p. 277)

☐ Blocks to Successful Meetings (p. 128)

☐ Clarifying Potential and Its Subelement, Structure (p. 132)

☐ Clarifying Potential and Its Subelement, Resources (p. 135)

☐ Program Evaluation: Short Form (p. 223)

Overhead Transparencies

☐ Welcome to the Model for Superior Facilitation (p. 265)

☐ Objectives for Half-Day Program: Introduction to Superior Facilitation (p. 269)

☐ Half-Day Program Flow (p. 272)

☐ The Model for Superior Facilitation (p. 276)

☐ The Meaning of Superior Facilitation (p. 277)

☐ The Model for Successful Meetings (p. 278)

An Introduction to Superior Facilitation

Objectives   The objectives of this program are to help participants understand the meaning of superior facilitation, to introduce *The Model for Superior Facilitation* and *The Model for Successful Meetings*, and to clarify the subelements in the model.

Materials Needed   You will require the following specific training materials to deliver this program:

- Participant Handouts
- Overhead Transparencies

Workshop Agenda

Introduction to Superior Facilitation	Minutes 3 hrs. 45	Start / Stop	Actual Start / Stop
Welcome and Administrative Details	10	9:00 / 9:10	_____ / _____
Program Overview	05	9:10 / 9:15	_____ / _____
Interactive Presentation: The Model for Superior Facilitation	10	9:15 / 9:25	_____ / _____
Clarifying the Model for Superior Facilitation	25	9:25 / 9:50	_____ / _____
Debrief	05	9:50 / 9:55	_____ / _____
Interactive Presentation: The First Competency, Understanding and Using the Meaning of Superior Facilitation	05	9:55 / 10:00	_____ / _____
Understanding the Meaning of Superior Facilitation	25	10:00 / 10:25	_____ / _____
Debrief	05	10:25 / 10:30	_____ / _____
Break	10	10:30 / 10:40	_____ / _____
Transition to the Second Competency, Understanding and Using the Model for Successful Meetings	05	10:40 / 10:45	_____ / _____
Blocks to Successful Meetings	25	10:45 / 11:10	_____ / _____
Debrief (and Introduce the Model for Successful Meetings)	15	11:10 / 11:25	_____ / _____
Transition to Subelements of the Model for Successful Meetings	05	11:25 / 11:30	_____ / _____
Clarifying Potential and Its Subelement, Structure	25	11:30 / 11:55	_____ / _____
Debrief	05	11:55 / 12:00	_____ / _____

Workshop Agenda

Introduction to Superior Facilitation	Minutes 3 hrs. 45	Start / Stop	Actual Start / Stop
Clarifying Potential and Its Subelement, Resources	25	12:00 / 12:25	_____ / _____
Debrief	05	12:25 / 12:30	_____ / _____
Review and Wrap-Up	10	12:30 / 12:40	_____ / _____
Program Evaluation: Short Form	05	12:40 / 12:45	_____ / _____

Program Flow

FACILITATOR COMMENTARY

00:10   **Welcome and Administrative Details**

 WELCOME the participants. Give title of program, its length, information on breaks and lunch. Briefly introduce yourself. Announce pertinent administrative details such as the location of restrooms, eating arrangements, telephones, how to get messages, smoking, etc.

 DISPLAY the overhead, *Welcome to the Model for Superior Facilitation* (p. 266).

00:05   **Program Overview**

 DISPLAY the overhead, *Objectives for Half-Day Program* (p. 267), and connect this program to any past facilitation training the participants have had and any future facilitation training scheduled.

 DISPLAY the overhead, *Half-Day Program Flow* (p. 272), and *REVIEW* the topics.

INTERACTIVE PRESENTATION

00:10   **The Model for Superior Facilitation**

 DISPLAY The Model for Superior Facilitation (p. 276) and *The Meaning of Superior Facilitation* (p. 277).

 EMPHASIZE that superior facilitation is results oriented. Describe briefly each element in the model. Identify *Understanding and Using the Meaning of Superior Facilitation* as the first competency in the model. (Refer to Chapter 2 for complete information about the model.)

LEARNING ACTIVITY

00:25   **Clarifying the Model for Superior Facilitation**

  DISTRIBUTE and *REVIEW* the exercise and its objectives, keeping the overhead of *The Model for Superior Facilitation* on screen during the exercise.

ASSIGN breakout rooms, if used, and assign time to complete exercise and return to general session.

 REMIND participants that they will be using the model in all future activities in the program (if you plan later programs).

00:05   **Debrief**

 Make sure the following ideas are brought out:

- Superior facilitation is any useful thing that any team member does or any designated facilitator does that helps a team have a successful meeting.

- Superior facilitation is based on the six competencies.

 REVIEW each of the six competencies.

 DISPLAY *The Model for Superior Facilitation* (p. 276) and *The Meaning of Superior Facilitation* (p. 277).

INTERACTIVE PRESENTATION

00:05   **The 1st Competency: Understanding and Using the Meaning of Superior Facilitation**

 DISPLAY *The Meaning of Superior Facilitation* (p. 277).

 EMPHASIZE that anyone can facilitate and does facilitate if he/she provides input that helps the team reach its goals and maintain or improve its competencies to meet and continue to meet its goals. Emphasize that superior facilitation is results oriented and disciplined.

LEARNING ACTIVITY

00:25   **Understanding the Meaning of Superior Facilitation**

 DISTRIBUTE the handout, *Understanding the Meaning of Superior Facilitation* (p. 126) and *REVIEW* the exercise and its objectives.

 ASSIGN breakout rooms, if used, and assign time to complete exercise and return to general session.

 REMIND participants that the definition of superior facilitation is the basis for what will be emphasized in the program and it is the definition which is a major guide in their learning how to become superior facilitators. Understanding the meaning of superior facilitation is the first of the six competencies for superior facilitation.

 DISPLAY The Meaning of Superior Facilitation (p. 277).

00:05   **Debrief**

Make sure the following ideas are brought out:

- Superior facilitation is based on *The Model for Superior Facilitation.*

- The model identifies six competencies of superior facilitation.

- The first competency is *Understanding the Meaning of Superior Facilitation.*

- The meaning of superior facilitation emphasizes facilitation that produces results.

 EMPHASIZE the distinction between facilitator and facilitation, i.e., anyone who makes a useful input facilitates, whether he/she is a designated facilitator or not.

 DISPLAY The Meaning of Superior Facilitation (p. 277) and *The Model for Superior Facilitation* (p. 276).

00:10   **Break**

00:05   **Transition to the 2nd Competency:**
                                         Understanding and Using the Model for Successful Meetings

 EMPHASIZE that superior facilitation is based on *The Model for Superior Facilitation.* The model identifies six competencies. The first competency is to understand and use the meaning of superior facilitation. The second competency is to understand and use *The Model for Successful Meetings.*

 DISPLAY The Meaning of Superior Facilitation (p. 277).

LEARNING ACTIVITY

00:25   **Blocks to Successful Meetings**

 DISTRIBUTE the handout, *Blocks to Successful Meetings* (p. 128) and *REVIEW* the exercise and its objectives.

 ASSIGN breakout rooms, if used, and assign time to complete the exercise and return to general session.

 REMIND participants that they are in the process of examining each of the six competencies identified in the *Model for Superior Facilitation.*

 REMIND participants that having in their minds just what a good meeting looks like is essential for superior facilitation and that you are going to develop such a model, using their own experience.

00:15   **Debrief**

The trainer first makes an interactive presentation to describe *The Model for Successful Meetings.* After the model has been presented, the trainer has each team present the results of the exercise. The trainer uses the information presented and (with the help of the group) assigns each item to one of the elements or subelements in the model.

Make sure the following ideas are brought out:

- Superior facilitation depends on our having a clear picture in our minds of what a successful meeting looks like.

- We already know from our own experience the kinds of things that block successful meetings.

- A successful meeting is created by avoiding these blocks.

 DISTRIBUTE the handout and *DISPLAY* the overhead, *The Model for Successful Meetings* (p. 278).

00:05   **Transition to Subelements in the Model for Successful Meetings**

 DISPLAY The Model for Successful Meetings (p. 278).

 REMIND participants that the model has six competencies. The second competency is *Understanding and Using the Model for Successful Meetings.* They have had an overview of the model. Now they will begin to look at the elements and subelements in greater detail.   In this exercise they will look at *Potential* and its subelement, *Structures.*

LEARNING ACTIVITY

00:25   **Clarifying Potential and Its Subelement, Structures**

 DISTRIBUTE the handout, *Clarifying Potential and Its Subelement, Structures* (p. 132) and *REVIEW* the exercise and its objectives.

 Assign breakout rooms, if used, and assign time to complete the exercise and return to general session.

 DISPLAY The Model for Superior Facilitation as you introduce the exercise.

00:05   **Debrief**

 HAVE each team put its chart up so that each chart is visible to all members of the training group. Starting with the first behavior listed, identify with the group behaviors from other charts that are essentially the same.

 DISCUSS why the behavior suggests a problem in structure. Repeat the process until all items are covered.

 DISCUSS any questions relating to structure that the teams identified.

LEARNING ACTIVITY

00:25   **Clarifying Potential and Its Subelement, Resources**

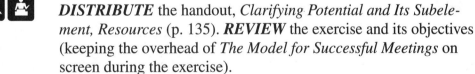 *DISTRIBUTE* the handout, *Clarifying Potential and Its Subelement, Resources* (p. 135). *REVIEW* the exercise and its objectives (keeping the overhead of *The Model for Successful Meetings* on screen during the exercise).

 ASSIGN breakout rooms, if used, and assign time to complete the exercise and return to general session.

 INDICATE that this exercise and the ones that follow have the purpose of explaining the subelements that go with each element in the model. In this exercise the subject is *potential* and its subelement *resources.*

 REMIND participants that understanding and using the model is the second of the six competencies used in superior facilitation.

00:05   **Debrief**

HAVE each team put its chart up so that each chart is visible to all members of the training group. Starting with the first behavior listed, identify with the group behaviors from other charts that are essentially the same.

DISCUSS why the behavior suggests a problem in resources. Repeat the process until all items are covered.

DISCUSS any questions relating to resources that the teams identified.

00:10   **Review and Wrap-Up**

USE the overheads that you have used earlier in the program to summarize the key learning points. Start, of course, with the program objectives.

- *Objectives for Half-Day Program: The Model for Superior Facilitation* (p. 267)

- *The Model for Superior Facilitation* (p. 276)

- *The Model for Successful Meetings* (p. 278)

00:05   **Program Evaluation**

If this program is a single event and is not tied to training that has gone before or training that will come after, you can use the *Program Evaluation: Short Form* (p. 223).

Notes

- _____
- _____
- _____
- _____
- _____
- _____
- _____
- _____
- _____
- _____
- _____

Chapter Six:

One-Day Facilitation Design

This chapter contains training designs for a one-day facilitation program—ready to go "as is" or to be tailored to meet your needs. The chapter is divided into four parts:

- Introduction

- Materials Needed

- Workshop Agenda

- Program Flow

"THE MODEL FOR SUPERIOR FACILITATION"

The one-day program has been designed to assist partic i-pants in understanding, *The Model for Superior Facilitation*, to familiarize participants with the six competencies of sup e-rior facilitation, and to give them the opportunity to practice facilitation and receive feedback. Topics covered include :

- The Meaning of Superior Facilitatio n

- Helping the Team Develop Its Potentia l

- Team Evaluation and Feedbac k

- Using Quality Communicatio n

Introduction

The one-day design is primarily intended as an introduction to facilitation. Some skill training and skill acquisition can be achieved. The one-day design should be followed with several additional training modules. Learning facilitation skills requires that individuals *facilitate* the meetings of teams. This kind of practice is best done with videotaping and replay. It must always be done with some sort of structured feedback. Practice and feedback require a number of considerations and time.

Materials Needed

The following materials are recommended for the one-day facilitation design. Page references indicate where masters for the materials are found elsewhere in this book. Unless otherwise noted:

- For overhead transparencies, you will need one transparency each.

- For other items, you will need one per participant, plus a few spares.

Participant Handouts

- ☐ The Model for Superior Facilitation (p. 276)
- ☐ The Model for Successful Meetings (p. 278)
- ☐ Quality Communication (p. 279)
- ☐ The Special Functions of Facilitation (p. 281)
- ☐ Types of Rational Tools (p. 282)
- ☐ Blocks to Successful Meetings (p. 128)
- ☐ Practicing Facilitation, Helping the Team Develop Its Potential (p. 153)
- ☐ Observation Sheet (Potential) (p. 156)
- ☐ Teem Meeting Evaluation Sheet (p. 176)
- ☐ Practicing Quality Communication (p. 178)
- ☐ Observation Sheet (Quality Communication) (p. 181)
- ☐ Understanding and Practicing Rational Tools (Developing Information and Ideas) (p. 194)
- ☐ Observation Sheet (Developing Information and Ideas) (p. 197)
- ☐ Review and Action Log (p. 218)
- ☐ Program Evaluation: Long Form (p. 224)

Overhead Transparencies

- ☐ Welcome to the Model for Superior Facilitation (p. 265)
- ☐ Objectives for One-Day Program (p. 270)
- ☐ One-Day Program Flow (p. 273)
- ☐ Program Norms (p. 275)
- ☐ The Model for Superior Facilitation (p. 276)
- ☐ The Meaning of Superior Facilitation (p. 277)
- ☐ The Model for Successful Meetings (p. 278)
- ☐ Quality Communication (p. 279)
- ☐ Special Functions of Facilitation (p. 281)
- ☐ Types of Rational Tools (p. 282)
- ☐ Tools for Generating Information and Ideas (p. 283)

The Model for Superior Facilitation

Objectives

The one-day program has been designed to assist participants in understanding *The Model for Superior Facilitation,* to familiarize participants with the six competencies of superior facilitation, and to give them the opportunity to practice facilitation and receive feedback.

Materials Needed

You will require the following specific training materials to deliver this program:

- Participant Handouts
- Visual Aids

Workshop Agenda

The Model for Superior Facilitation	7 hrs 40 min.	Start / Stop 8:00 / 3:40	Actual Start / Stop
Welcome and Administrative Details	10	8:00 / 8:10	_____ / _____
Program Overview	10	8:10 / 8:20	_____ / _____
Program Norms	05	8:20 / 8:25	_____ / _____
Introductions	10	8:25 / 8:35	_____ / _____
Interactive Presentation: The Model for Superior Facilitation	10	8:35 / 8:45	_____ / _____
Interactive Presentation: The 1st Competency, Understanding and Using the Meaning of Superior Facilitation	05	8:45 / 8:50	_____ / _____
Transition to the 2nd Competency, Understanding and Using the Model for Successful Meetings	05	8:50 / 8:55	_____ / _____
Blocks to Successful Meetings	25	8:55 / 9:20	_____ / _____
Debrief (Introduce the Model for Successful Meetings)	15	9:20 / 9:35	_____ / _____
Transition to Practicing Facilitation	05	9:35 / 9:40	_____ / _____
Break	10	9:40 / 9:50	_____ / _____
Practicing Facilitation, Helping the Team Develop Its Potential	1:15	9:50 / 11:05	_____ / _____
Debrief	05	11:05 / 11:10	_____ / _____

The Model for Superior Facilitation	7 hrs 40 min.	Start / Stop 8:00 / 3:40	Actual Start / Stop
Interactive Presentation: The 3rd Competency, Understanding and Using Team Evaluation and Feedback	10	11:10 / 11:20	_____ / _____
Review/Preview	05	11:20 / 11:25	_____ / _____
Lunch	45	11:25 / 12:10	_____ / _____
Transition to the 4th Competency, Using Quality Communication	05	12:10 / 12:15	_____ / _____
Practicing Quality Communication	1:15	12:15 / 1:30	_____ / _____
Debrief	05	1:30 / 1:35	_____ / _____
Interactive Presentation: the 5th Competency, Understanding and Using the Special Functions of Facilitation	10	1:35 / 1:45	_____ / _____
Break	10	1:45 / 1:55	_____ / _____
Transition to the 6th Competency, Understanding and Using Rational Tools	05	1:55 / 2:00	_____ / _____
Understanding and Practicing Rational Tools (Developing Information and Ideas)	1:00	2:00 / 3:00	_____ / _____
Debrief	05	3:00 / 3:05	_____ / _____
Review and Action Logs	10	3:05 / 3:15	_____ / _____
Program Review and Wrap-Up	10	3:15 / 3:25	_____ / _____
Program Evaluation: Long Form	15	3:25 / 3:40	_____ / _____

Program Flow

FACILITATOR COMMENTARY

00:10   **Welcome and Administrative Details**

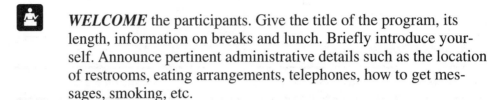 *WELCOME* the participants. Give the title of the program, its length, information on breaks and lunch. Briefly introduce yourself. Announce pertinent administrative details such as the location of restrooms, eating arrangements, telephones, how to get messages, smoking, etc.

DISPLAY the overhead, *Welcome to the Model for Superior Facilitation* (p. 265).

00:10   **Program Overview**

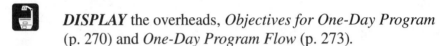 *DISPLAY* the overheads, *Objectives for One-Day Program* (p. 270) and *One-Day Program Flow* (p. 273).

EXPLAIN the program objectives, one-day program flow, and connect this program to any past facilitation training that participants have had and any future facilitation training scheduled.

00:05   **Program Norms**

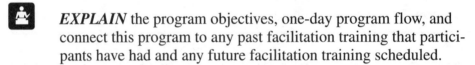 *EXPLAIN* that norms set the way the program will be conducted and how participants are expected to perform.

DISPLAY the overhead, *Program Norms* (p. 275).

00:10   **Introductions**

STRUCTURE the introduction so that each participant gives their name, job, organization, and previous experience in facilitation training programs. This activity is only appropriate when the training group is relatively small.

INTERACTIVE PRESENTATION

00:10   **The Model for Superior Facilitation**

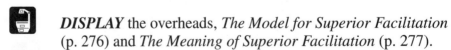 *DISPLAY* the overheads, *The Model for Superior Facilitation* (p. 276) and *The Meaning of Superior Facilitation* (p. 277).

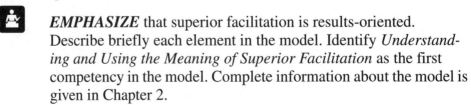 *EMPHASIZE* that superior facilitation is results-oriented. Describe briefly each element in the model. Identify *Understanding and Using the Meaning of Superior Facilitation* as the first competency in the model. Complete information about the model is given in Chapter 2.

INTERACTIVE PRESENTATION

00:05   **The 1st Competency: Understanding and
Using the Meaning of Superior Facilitation**

 DISPLAY the overhead, *The Meaning of Superior Facilitation*
(p. 277), keeping it on the screen through the next transition.

 EMPHASIZE that anyone can facilitate and does facilitate if he/
she provides input that helps the team reach its goals and maintain
or improve its competencies to meet and continue to meet its goals.
Emphasize that superior facilitation is results-oriented and disciplined.

00:05   **Transition to the 2nd Competency:
Understanding and Using the Model for Successful Meetings**

 EMPHASIZE that superior facilitation is based on *The Model for
Superior Facilitation*. The model identifies six competencies. The
first competency is to understand and use the meaning of superior
facilitation. The second competency is to understand and use *The
Model for Successful Meetings*.

LEARNING ACTIVITY

00:25   **Blocks to Successful Meetings**

 DISTRIBUTE Blocks to Successful Meetings (p. 128) and
REVIEW the exercise and its objectives.

 ASSIGN breakout rooms, if used, and assign time to complete the
exercise and return to general session.

 REMIND participants that they are in the process of examining
each of the six competencies identified in *The Model for Superior
Facilitation*, that having in their minds just what a good meeting
looks like is essential for superior facilitation, and that you are
going to develop such a model, using their own experience.

GROUP ACTIVITY

00:15   **Debrief (Introduce the Model for Successful Meetings)**

 MAKE an interactive presentation to describe *The Model for Successful Meetings.*

 HAVE each team present the results of the exercise. Use the information presented and (with the help of the group) assign each item to one of the elements or subelements in the model. Make sure the following ideas are brought out:

- Superior facilitation depends on our having a clear picture in our minds of what a successful meeting looks like.

- We already know from our own experience the kinds of things that block successful meetings.

- A successful meeting is created by avoiding these blocks.

DISTRIBUTE the handout and *DISPLAY* the overhead, *The Model for Successful Meetings* (p. 278).

FACILITATOR COMMENTARY

00:05   **Transition to Practicing Facilitation**

 TELL participants that they have been introduced to *The Model for Superior Facilitation* and have reviewed the first two competencies in the model for superior facilitation. Now they are going to practice using the first two competencies in the next exercise.

00:10   **Break**

LEARNING ACTIVITY

01:15   **Practicing Facilitation: Helping the Team Develop Its Potential**

 DISTRIBUTE Practicing Facilitation: Helping the Team Develop Its Potential (p. 153) and *REVIEW* the exercise and its objectives.

 ASSIGN breakout rooms, if used, and assign time to complete the exercise and return to general session.

 DISPLAY the overhead, *The Model for Superior Facilitation* (p. 276), keeping it on screen as you set up this exercise.

 REMIND participants that they are learning the six competencies required for superior facilitation and they are presently working on the second competency, *Using the Model for Successful Meetings.*

EMPHASIZE that participants will focus on the first element in the model, *Potential*, and practice helping a team develop and use resources and structure.

 DISTRIBUTE copies of the *Observation Sheet (Potential)* (p. 156) to ensure that participants understand how the sheet in the exercise will be used.

GROUP ACTIVITY

00:05   **Debrief**

 REVIEW each team's key learning points which they have brought back from the exercise.

 CONDUCT a general discussion about *The Model for Successful Meetings* and the function of helping a team develop and use resources and structures.

INTERACTIVE PRESENTATION

00:10   **The 3rd Competency: Understanding and
                             Using Team Evaluation and Feedback**

 INTRODUCE participants to the third competency, *Understanding and Using Team Feedback*.

 REFER them to the two tools for evaluating a meeting: *Program Norms* (p. 275) and the *Team Meeting Evaluation Sheet* (p. 176). Use the Learning Activity, *Understanding and Using Team Evaluation and Feedback* (p. 173) as a resource.

 TELL participants that they will be using the *Team Evaluation and Feedback Sheet* during the rest of the training program.

00:05   **Review/Preview**

 INDICATE that participants have been introduced to *The Model for Superior Facilitation* and the first three competencies.

 DISPLAY the overhead, *The Model for Superior Facilitation* (p. 276).

 INDICATE that in the afternoon the topics will be the remaining competencies in the model.

00:45   **Lunch**

00:05   **Transition to the 4th Competency, Understanding and Using Quality Communication**

 INDICATE that participants are now going to look at the fourth competency, *Quality Communication*, and that in the next exercise they will practice quality communication and receive feedback on their performance.

LEARNING ACTIVITY

01:15   **Practicing Quality Communication**

DISTRIBUTE *Practicing Quality Communication* (p. 178) and *REVIEW* the exercise and its objectives.

ASSIGN breakout rooms, if used, and assign the time to complete the exercise and return to general session.

DISPLAY the overhead, *The Model for Superior Facilitation* (p. 276) on the screen.

REMIND participants that they are learning the six competencies required for superior facilitation. They are working on the fourth competency, *Modeling and Using Quality Communication*.

DISPLAY the overhead, *Quality Communication* (p. 279) and review the characteristics of quality communication.

DISTRIBUTE and *REVIEW* the *Observation Sheet (Quality Communication)* (p. 181) that the observer/timer will use for this exercise so that everyone is clear about what is being observed.

DISTRIBUTE the handout and *DISPLAY* the overhead, *Quality Communication* (p. 279).

00:05   **Debrief**

REVIEW examples that each team brings back to the general session, which illustrate when members of a team did not use quality communication during the practice session.

DISCUSS these examples and the reasons for the poor communication, i.e., was not balanced, or concrete, or respectful, or relevant.

| 00:10 | **Break** |

Interactive Presentation

00:10   **The 5th Competency: Understanding and Using the Special Functions of Facilitation**

 DISTRIBUTE the handout and *DISPLAY* the overhead, *Special Functions of Facilitation* (p. 281).

 REVIEW each of the special functions briefly. (See Chapter 2 for more information on the functions.)

 There is not enough time in a one-day program to practice these functions. Each of the functions can be made the topic of follow-up programs. Trainers can also use information on the functions as handouts for participants.

00:05   **Transition to the 6th Competency, Understanding and Using Rational Tools**

 DISPLAY the overhead, *The Model for Superior Facilitation* (p. 276).

 SHOW participants that they have covered the first five competencies and are now going to practice the sixth competency.

 DISPLAY the overhead, *Types of Rational Tools* (p. 282) to introduce the kinds of rational tools that facilitators must master.

 INDICATE that they will practice using tools to develop information and ideas and receive feedback on their performance.

Learning Activity

01:00   **Understanding and Practicing Rational Tools (Developing Information and Ideas)**

 DISTRIBUTE Understanding and Practicing Rational Tools (Developing Information and Ideas) (p. 194) and *REVIEW* the exercise and its objectives.

 ASSIGN breakout rooms, if used, and assign time to complete the exercise and return to general session.

 DISPLAY the overhead, *The Model for Superior Facilitation* (p. 276) on the screen.

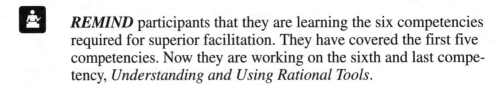

REMIND participants that they are learning the six competencies required for superior facilitation. They have covered the first five competencies. Now they are working on the sixth and last competency, *Understanding and Using Rational Tools*.

DISTRIBUTE the handout and **DISPLAY** the overhead, *Types of Rational Tools* (p. 282).

REVIEW the three kinds of tools. Emphasize that they will be working on the first kinds of tools; ones for developing information and ideas.

DISPLAY the overhead, *Tools for Generating Information and Ideas* (p. 283).

REVIEW these tools.

DISTRIBUTE and **EXPLAIN** how the *Observation Sheet (Developing Information and Ideas)* (p. 197) will be used in this exercise so that team members understand what is being observed.

00:05   **Debrief**

Each team will bring back to the general session questions about the tools that they have practiced using. They also bring back information about how they might use the tools.

REVIEW and respond to questions and review possible uses of the tools.

00:10   **Review and Action Logs**

DISTRIBUTE and **HAVE** participants complete a copy of the *Review and Action Log* (p. 218) to record their key learnings.

DISCUSS key learning points and jointly complete the logs, (as time permits for each team).

EMPHASIZE that the logs should be referred to after a few days to help remind participants of what they learned about superior facilitation and to encourage them to put their learning into practice.

00:10   **Program Review and Wrap-Up**

REVIEW program objectives, *The Model for Superior Facilitation*, and the six competencies.

DISPLAY the overheads, *Objectives for One-Day Program* (p. 270) and *The Model for Superior Facilitation* (p. 276).

00:15   **Program Evaluation**

DISTRIBUTE copies of the *Program Evaluation: Long Form* (p. 224) to each participant.

Notes
- _____
- _____
- _____
- _____
- _____
- _____
- _____
- _____
- _____
- _____
- _____
- _____
- _____
- _____
- _____
- _____
- _____
- _____
- _____
- _____
- _____

Chapter Seven:

Two-Day Facilitation Design

This chapter contains training designs for a two-day facilitation program—ready to go "as is" or to be tailored to meet your needs. The chapter is divided into five parts:

- Introduction

- Materials Needed

- Workshop Agenda

- Program Flow: Day One

- Program Flow: Day Two

"THE MODEL FOR SUPERIOR FACILITATION"

This two-day program has been designed to assist participants to understand *The Model for Superior Facilitation* and to familiarize participants with the six competencies of superior facilitation. Participants will be given the opportunity to :

- Practice facilitation.

- Receive feedback.

- Plan how to reinforce their learning.

Participants will be involved in a number of skill building exercises and participate in several videotaped practice inter-actions in which they will apply the superior facilitation com-petencies that are identified in *The Model for Superior Facilitation*.

Introduction

The two-day design permits participants to do a great deal more than just learn about facilitation. They are involved in a number of skill building exercises, and they participate in several videotaped practice interactions in which they apply the superior facilitation competencies identified in *The Model for Superior Facilitation*. The two-day design provides a good foundation in facilitation skills that can be enhanced with follow-up training of one hour or more. For example, even in a two-day design, the number of practice facilitation rounds for each participant are still limited. For example, there is not enough time for all participants to practice all of the special facilitation functions like resource, teacher, challenger, and mediator. Also, there is not enough time for all participants to practice the use of all of the rational tools, like the Gallery Method, Plus-and-Minus Technique, Priority Analysis, Flowcharting, Cause-and-Effect Diagrams, and Pareto Charts. Follow-up programs can offer participants additional practice in all of these areas.

Materials Needed

These are the materials recommended for the two-day facilitation design. Page references indicate where masters for the materials are found elsewhere in this book. Unless otherwise noted:

- For overhead transparencies, you will need one transparency each.

- For other items, you will need one per participant, plus a few spares.

Participant Handouts

- ☐ The Model for Superior Facilitation (p. 276)
- ☐ The Meaning of Superior Facilitation (p. 277)
- ☐ The Model for Successful Meetings (p. 278)
- ☐ Quality Communication (p. 279)
- ☐ Special Functions of Facilitation (p. 281)
- ☐ Types of Rational Tools (p. 282)
- ☐ Clarifying the Model for Superior Facilitation (p. 124)
- ☐ Understanding the Meaning of Superior Facilitation (p. 126)
- ☐ Blocks to Successful Meetings (p. 128)
- ☐ Clarifying Potential and Its Subelement, Structure (p. 132)
- ☐ Clarifying Potential and Its Subelement, Resources (p. 135)
- ☐ Practicing Facilitation, Helping the Team Develop Its Potential (p. 153)
- ☐ Observation Sheet (Potential) (p. 156)
- ☐ Practicing Facilitation, Helping Teams Perform (Communication) (p. 159)
- ☐ Understanding and Using Team Evaluation and Feedback (p. 174)
- ☐ Team Meeting Evaluation Sheet (p. 176)
- ☐ Practicing Quality Communication (p. 178)
- ☐ Observation Sheet (Quality Communication) (p. 181)
- ☐ Understanding and Practicing the Special Functions of Facilitation (p. 183)
- ☐ Observation Sheet (Special Functions) (p. 190)

- ☐ Understanding and Practicing Rational Tools (Developing Information and Ideas) (p. 194)
- ☐ Observation Sheet (Developing Information and Ideas) (p. 197)
- ☐ Practicing Facilitation, Putting It All Together (p. 211)
- ☐ Observation Sheet (Putting It All Together) (p. 197)
- ☐ Review and Action Logs (p. 218)
- ☐ Program Evaluation: Long Form (p. 224)
- ☐ Objectives for the Two-Day Program (p. 271)
- ☐ Two-Day Program Flow (p. 274)
- ☐ Program Norms (p. 275)
- ☐ Tools for Generating Information and Ideas (p. 283)

Overhead Transparencies

- ☐ Welcome to the Model for Superior Facilitation (p. 265)
- ☐ Objectives for Two-Day Program (p. 271)
- ☐ Two-Day Program Flow (p. 274)
- ☐ Program Norms (p. 275)
- ☐ The Model for Superior Facilitation (p. 276)
- ☐ The Meaning of Superior Facilitation (p. 277)
- ☐ The Model for Successful Meetings (p. 278)
- ☐ Quality Communication (p. 279)
- ☐ Developing Understanding (p. 280)
- ☐ Special Functions of Facilitation (p. 281)
- ☐ Types of Rational Tools (p. 282)
- ☐ Tools for Generating Information and Ideas (p. 283)
-    Review and Action Teams (p. 286)

The Model for Superior Facilitation

Objectives

The training objectives for the two-day design are to assist partici-pants to understand *The Model for Superior Facilitation*, to famil-iarize participants with the six competencies of superior facilitation. Participants will be given the opportunity to practice facilitation, receive feedback, and plan how they will continue to reinforce their learning after the program.

Materials Needed

You will require the following specific training materials to deliver this program:

- Participant Handouts
- Overhead Transparencies

Workshop Agenda

Day One: The Model for Superior Facilitation	8 hrs. 45 min.	Start / Stop 8:00 / 4:45	Actual Start / Stop
Welcome and Administrative Details	10	8:00 / 8:10	_____ / _____
Program Overview	10	8:10 / 8:20	_____ / _____
Program Norms	05	8:20 / 8:25	_____ / _____
Introductions	10	8:25 / 8:35	_____ / _____
Organize R & A Teams and Introduce Review and Action Logs	15	8:35 / 8:50	_____ / _____
Interactive Presentation: The Model for Superior Facilitation	10	8:50 / 9:00	_____ / _____
Clarifying the Model for Superior Facilitation	25	9:00 / 9:25	_____ / _____
Debrief	10	9:25 / 9:35	_____ / _____
Interactive Presentation: The 1st Competency, Understanding and Using The Meaning of Superior Facilitation	05	9:35 / 9:40	_____ / _____
Understanding the Meaning of Superior Facilitation	25	9:40 / 10:05	_____ / _____
Debrief	05	10:05 / 10:10	_____ / _____
Break	10	10:10 / 10:20	_____ / _____

Day One: The Model for Superior Facilitation	8 hrs. 45 min.	Start / Stop 8:00 / 4:45	Actual Start / Stop
Transition to the 2nd Competency, Understanding and Using the Model for Successful Meetings	05	10:20 / 10:25	_____ / _____
Blocks to Successful Meetings	25	10:25 / 10:50	_____ / _____
Debrief (Introduce the Model for Successful Meetings)	15	10:50 / 11:05	_____ / _____
Clarifying Potential and Its Subelement, Structures	25	11:05 / 11:30	_____ / _____
Debrief	10	11:30 / 11:40	_____ / _____
Clarifying Potential and Its Subelement, Resources	25	11:40 / 12:05	_____ / _____
Debrief	10	12:05 / 12:15	_____ / _____
Review/Preview	05	12:15 / 12:20	_____ / _____
Lunch	45	12:20 / 1:05	_____ / _____
Practicing Facilitation, Helping the Team Develop Its Potential	1:15	1:05 / 2:20	_____ / _____
Debrief	05	2:20 / 2:25	_____ / _____
Transition to the 2nd Element in the Model for Successful Meetings	05	2:25 / 2:30	_____ / _____
Practicing Facilitation, Helping Teams Perform (Focus on Communication)	1:00	2:30 / 3:30	_____ / _____
Debrief	10	3:30 / 3:40	_____ / _____
Transition to the 3rd Competency, Understanding and Using Team Evaluation and Feedback	05	3:40 / 3:45	_____ / _____
Understanding and Using Team Evaluation and Feedback	30	3:45 / 4:15	_____ / _____
Debrief	10	4:15 / 4:25	_____ / _____
Complete Review and Action Logs	10	4:25 / 4:35	_____ / _____
Review/Preview	10	4:35 / 4:45	_____ / _____

Workshop Agenda

Day Two: The Model for Superior Facilitation	8 hrs.	Start / Stop 8:00 / 4:00	Actual Start / Stop
Introduction	05	8:00 / 8:05	_____ / _____
R & A Team Activity: R & A Logs	20	8:05 / 8:30	_____ / _____
Transition to the 4th Competency, Understanding and Using Quality Communication	05	8:30 / 8:35	_____ / _____
Practicing Quality Communication	1:15	8:35 / 9:50	_____ / _____
Debrief	10	9:50 / 10:00	_____ / _____
Break	10	10:00 / 10:10	_____ / _____
Interactive Presentation: The 5th Competency, Understanding and Using the Special Functions of Facilitation	10	10:10 / 10:20	_____ / _____
Understanding and Practicing the Special Functions of Facilitation	1:00	10:20 / 11:20	_____ / _____
Debrief	10	11:20 / 11:30	_____ / _____
Lunch	45	11:30 / 12:15	_____ / _____
Transition to The 6th Competency, Understanding and Using Rational Tools	05	12:15 / 12:20	_____ / _____
Understanding and Practicing Rational Tools (Developing Information and Ideas)	1:00	12:20 / 1:20	_____ / _____
Debrief	10	1:20 / 1:30	_____ / _____
Break	10	1:30 / 1:40	_____ / _____
Practicing Facilitation, Putting It All Together	1:00	1:40 / 2:40	_____ / _____
Debrief	10	2:40 / 2:50	_____ / _____
R & A Team Activity, R & A Logs	20	2:50 / 3:10	_____ / _____
Program Review and Wrap-Up	15	3:10 / 3:25	_____ / _____
Program Evaluation, Long Form	15	3:25 / 4:00	_____ / _____

Program Flow: Day One

FACILITATOR COMMENTARY

00:10   **Welcome and Administrative Details**

WELCOME the participants. Give title of program, its length, information on breaks and lunch. Briefly introduce yourself. Announce pertinent administrative details such as the location of restrooms, eating arrangements, telephones, how to get messages, smoking, etc.

DISPLAY the overhead, *Welcome to the Model for Superior Facilitation* (p. 265).

00:10   **Program Overview**

DISPLAY the overheads, *Objectives for Two-Day Program* (p. 271) *and Two-Day Program Flow* (p. 274).

EXPLAIN the program objectives, two-day program flow, and connect this program to any past facilitation training that participants have had and any future facilitation training scheduled.

00:05   **Program Norms**

EXPLAIN that norms set the way the program will be conducted and how participants are expected to perform.

DISPLAY the overhead, *Program Norms* (p. 275).

00:10   **Introductions**

STRUCTURE introductions by such things as having each participant give name, job, organization, and previous experience in facilitation training programs. (This activity is only appropriate when the training group is relatively small.)

00:15   **Organize Review and Action Teams and Introduce Review and Action Logs**

DISPLAY the overhead, *Review and Action Teams* (p. 286).

EXPLAIN the purpose of the teams. Make sure you have several logs for each participant. *DISTRIBUTE* at least three *Review and Action Logs* (p. 218) to each participant at this time. Whenever possible, teams should continue to meet after the program.

 EXPLAIN that the *Review and Action Log* is to be used throughout the program for participants to record what they have learned and how they might use what they have learned. Also, *Action and Review Logs* are used in the Review and Action Teams to identify key learning points, reinforce learning, and identify opportunities to apply what has been learned.

 It is easiest to have the participants seated initially with their Review and Action Teams on the first day, even if you change seating on the following day.

INTERACTIVE PRESENTATION

00:10   **The Model for Superior Facilitation**

 DISPLAY the overheads, *The Model for Superior Facilitation* (p. 276) and *The Meaning of Superior Facilitation* (p. 277).

EMPHASIZE that superior facilitation is results-oriented. Describe briefly each element in the model.

IDENTIFY *Understanding and Using the Meaning of Superior Facilitation* as the first competency in the model. Complete information about the model is given in Chapter 2.

LEARNING ACTIVITY

00:25   **Clarifying the Model for Superior Facilitation**

 DISTRIBUTE *Clarifying the Model for Superior Facilitation* (p. 124) and *REVIEW* the exercise and its objectives.

 ASSIGN breakout rooms, if used, and assign time to complete the exercise and return to general session.

 DISPLAY the overhead, *The Model for Superior Facilitation* (p. 276), on screen during the exercise.

 REMIND participants that they will be using the model in all future activities in the program.

00:10   **Debrief**

 DISCUSS the exercise and make sure the following ideas are brought out:

- Superior facilitation is any useful thing that any team member does or any designated facilitator does that helps a team have a successful meeting.

- Superior facilitation is based on the six competencies.

 REVIEW each of the six competencies.

INTERACTIVE PRESENTATION

00:05   **The First Competency, Understanding and Using the Meaning of Superior Facilitation**

 DISPLAY the overhead, *The Meaning of Superior Facilitation* (p. 277).

 EMPHASIZE that anyone can facilitate and does facilitate if he/she provides input that helps the team reach its goals and maintain or improve its competencies to meet and continue to meet its goals. Emphasize that superior facilitation is results-oriented and disciplined.

LEARNING ACTIVITY

00:25   **Understanding the Meaning of Superior Facilitation**

 DISTRIBUTE the handout, *Understanding the Meaning of Superior Facilitation* (p. 126) and *REVIEW* the exercise and its objectives.

 ASSIGN breakout rooms, if used, and assign time to complete the exercise and return to general session.

 REMIND participants that the definition of superior facilitation is the basis for what will be emphasized in the program, and it is the definition which is a major guide to their learning how to become superior facilitators. Understanding the meaning of superior facilitation is the first of the six competencies for superior facilitation.

 DISPLAY the overhead, *The Meaning of Superior Facilitation* (p. 277).

00:05   **Debrief**

DISCUSS the exercise and make sure the following ideas are brought out:

- Superior facilitation is based on *The Model for Superior Facilitation.*

- The model identifies six competencies of superior facilitation.

- The first competency is *Understanding the Meaning of Superior Facilitation.*

- The meaning of superior facilitation emphasizes facilitation that produces results.

EMPHASIZE the distinction between facilitator and facilitation, i.e., anyone who makes a useful input facilitates, whether he/she is a designated facilitator or not.

DISPLAY the overhead, *The Model for Superior Facilitation* (p. 276).

00:10   **Break**

00:05   **Transition to the 2nd Competency:**
Understanding and Using the Model for Successful Meetings

EMPHASIZE that superior facilitation is based on *The Model for Superior Facilitation*. The model identifies six competencies. The first competency is to *Understand and Use the Meaning of Superior Facilitation*. The second competency is to understand and use *The Model for Successful Meetings*.

DISPLAY the overhead, *The Meaning of Superior Facilitation* (p. 277).

LEARNING ACTIVITY

00:25   **Exercise 3: Blocks to Successful Meetings**

DISTRIBUTE the handout, *Blocks to Successful Meetings* (p. 128) and *REVIEW* the exercise and its objectives.

ASSIGN breakout rooms, if used, and assign time to complete exercise and return to general session.

REMIND participants that they are in the process of examining each of the six competencies identified in *The Model for Superior Facilitation.*

REMIND participants that having in their minds just what a good meeting looks like is essential for superior facilitation and that you are going to develop such a model, using their own experience.

00:15   **Debrief (Introduce the Model for Successful Meetings)**

 MAKE an interactive presentation to describe *The Model for Successful Meetings*. After the model has been presented, have each team present the results of the exercise. Use the information presented and (with the help of the group) assign each item to one of the elements or subelements in the model.

Make sure the following ideas are brought out:

- Superior facilitation depends on our having a clear picture in our minds of what a successful meeting looks like.

- We already know from our own experience the kinds of things that block successful meetings.

- A successful meeting is created by avoiding these blocks.

 DISTRIBUTE the handout and *DISPLAY* the overhead:

- *The Model for Successful Meetings* (p. 278).

LEARNING ACTIVITY

00:25   **Clarifying Potential and Its Subelement, Structure**

 DISTRIBUTE the handout, *Clarifying Potential and Its Subelement, Structure* (p. 132) and *REVIEW* the exercise and its objectives.

 *ASSIGN* breakout rooms, if used, and assign time to complete exercise and return to general session.

 DISPLAY the overhead, *The Model for Superior Facilitation* (p. 276).

 REMIND participants that they are learning the six competencies required for superior facilitation. The second competency is *Understanding and Using the Model for Successful Meetings*. They have had an overview of *The Model for Successful Meetings*. Now they will begin to look at each of the elements and subelements in greater detail.

00:10   **Debrief**

HAVE each team put its chart up so that each chart is visible to all members of the training group.

- Starting with the first behavior listed, identify with the group behaviors from other charts that are essentially the same.

- Discuss why the behavior suggests a problem in structure. Repeat the process until all items are covered.

- Discuss questions that the teams identified related to structure.

LEARNING ACTIVITY

00:25   **Clarifying Potential and Its Subelement, Resources**

DISTRIBUTE the handout, *Clarifying Potential and Its Subelement, Resources* (p. 135) and *REVIEW* the exercise and its objectives, keeping the overhead of *The Model for Successful Meetings* on screen during the exercise.

ASSIGN breakout rooms, if used, and assign time to complete the exercise and return to general session.

REMIND participants that understanding and using the model is the second of the six competencies used in superior facilitation. In this exercise the subject is *Potential* and its subelement *Resources*.

00:10   **Debrief**

Have each team put its chart up so that each chart is visible to all members of the training group.

- Starting with the first behavior listed, identify with the group behaviors from other charts that are essentially the same.

- Discuss why the behavior suggests a problem in resources. Repeat the process until all items are covered.

- Discuss any questions that the teams identified related to resources.

00:05   **Review/Preview**

DISPLAY the overheads, *Objectives for Two-Day Program* (p. 271) and *Two-Day Program Flow* (p. 274) to review program objectives.

DISTRIBUTE copies of *The Model for Superior Facilitation* (p. 276) and *The Meaning of Superior Facilitation* (p. 277) to review the competencies of *The Superior Facilitation Model.*

 EMPHASIZE that the group has been working on the first two competencies and will continue working on the second competency, *Understanding and Using the Model for Successful Meetings*, after lunch.

00:45   **Lunch**

LEARNING ACTIVITY

1:15   **Practicing Facilitation,
Helping the Team Develop Its Potential**

 DISTRIBUTE the handout, *Practicing Facilitation, Helping the Team Develop Its Potential* (p. 153) and *REVIEW* the exercise and its objectives.

 ASSIGN breakout rooms, if used, and assign time to complete the exercise and return to general session.

 DISPLAY the overhead, *The Model for Superior Facilitation* (p. 276), on the screen.

 REMIND participants that they are learning the six competencies required for superior facilitation and are presently working on the second competency, *Using the Model for Successful Meetings.*

 DISPLAY the overhead, *The Model for Successful Meetings* (p. 276), on the screen as you set up this exercise.

 EMPHASIZE that participants will focus on the first element in the model, *Potential*, and practice helping a team develop and use resources and structure.

 DISTRIBUTE and go over the *Observation Sheet (Potential)* (p. 156) to ensure that participants are clear how they will use the sheet in the exercise.

00:05   **Debrief**

REVIEW each team's three key learning points that have been brought back from the exercise. Conduct a general discussion about *The Model for Successful Meetings* and the function of helping a team develop and use resources and structures.

00:05   **Transition to the 2nd Element in Successful Meetings, Performance**

DISPLAY the overhead, *The Model for Successful Meetings* (p. 278).

TELL participants that they have reviewed the first element, *Potential*, and are now going to review the second element, *Performance*.

REVIEW the meaning of communication and rational tools. Within *Performance* there are three subelements. Show how these three elements determine how a team interacts and does work during a meeting. Chapter 2 is your resource for this information. Indicate that in the next exercise, participants will practice facilitating a team's communication.

LEARNING ACTIVITY

01:00   **Practicing Facilitation, Helping Teams Perform (Communication)**

DISTRIBUTE the handout, *Practicing Facilitation, Helping Teams Perform (Communication)* (p. 159) and *REVIEW* the exercise and its objectives.

ASSIGN breakout rooms, if used, and assign time to complete the exercise and return to general session.

DISPLAY the overhead, *The Model for Superior Facilitation* (p. 276) on the screen as you set up this exercise.

REMIND participants that they are learning the six competencies identified in *The Model for Superior Facilitation*. They have learned the meaning of the first competency, *Understanding and Using the Meaning of Superior Facilitation*. They are presently working on *Understanding and Using the Model for Successful Meetings*. They have covered the first element in the model, *Potential* and are now working on the second element, *Performance*.

EMPHASIZE that in the current exercise participants will focus on the first subelement of Performance, *Communication*. This exercise gives participants the chance to use the criteria of quality communication by observing their team members during a discussion.

00:10   **Debrief**

REVIEW and discuss each of the examples of poor communication that the teams have observed during the exercise.

00:05   **Transition to the 3rd Competency,
Understanding and Using Team Evaluation and Feedback**

DISPLAY the overhead, *The Model for Superior Facilitation* (p. 276) and show participants how they are proceeding through the six competencies. They have covered the first two and are now going to look at the third one.

TELL participants that they will be evaluating their team's performance during the rest of the training program.

LEARNING ACTIVITY

00:30   **Understanding and Using Team Evaluation and Feedback**

DISTRIBUTE the handouts, *Understanding and Using Team Evaluation and Feedback* (p. 174) and *Developing Understanding* (p. 280).

REVIEW the exercise and its objectives.

ASSIGN breakout rooms, if used, and assign time to complete the exercise and return to general session.

DISPLAY the overhead, *The Model for Superior Facilitation* (p. 276).

REMIND participants that they are learning the six competencies required for superior facilitation. Now they are working on the third competency, *Understanding and Using Evaluation and Feedback*. Review the meaning of evaluation and feedback. Information on this subject is found in Chapter 2.

00:10   **Debrief**

Each team will bring back to the general session their meeting norms and any questions they have about the process of evaluating team performance and helping teams use feedback on their performance to improve their meetings.

DISTRIBUTE and *EMPHASIZE* that participants will begin to use their *Program Norms* (p. 275) and the *Team Meeting Evaluation Sheet* (p. 176) to evaluate and improve the way their teams meet and work together during the remainder of the workshop.

00:10   **Complete Review and Action Logs**

REFER to the copies of the *Review and Action Log* (p. 218) that were previously distributed to each participant. Remind participants that logs will be used with their Review and Action Teams at the beginning of Day Two.

00:10   **Review/Preview**

DISTRIBUTE copies of the *Objectives for Two-Day Program* (p. 271) and *The Two-Day Program Flow* (p. 274).

REVIEW the objectives and topics to be covered in day two.

DISPLAY the overhead, *The Model for Superior Facilitation* (p. 276) and review the competencies covered and the ones that will be covered in day two.

Notes
- _____
- _____
- _____
- _____
- _____
- _____
- _____
- _____
- _____
- _____
- _____
- _____
- _____

Program Flow: Day Two

FACILITATOR COMMENTARY

00:05   **Introduction**

 INDICATE that participants will first meet in their Review and Action Teams to review their key learning points from day one and discuss how they can apply what they have learned. After this activity the program will continue to examine the six competencies for superior facilitation.

00:20   **Review and Action Team Activity: Review and Action Logs**

 REMIND participants that the purpose of the *Review and Action Log* is to help participants share and reinforce their learning and to develop personal resources for continued learning and application.

 INSTRUCT Review and Action Teams to:

• Have each member share his/her Review and Action Log.

• Clarify key learning points.

• Identify and discuss applications of what has been learned.

00:05   **Transition to 4th Competency:**
                             Understanding and Using Quality Communication

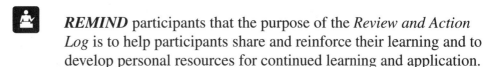 *DISPLAY* the overhead, *The Model for Superior Facilitation* (p. 276) and *INDICATE* that participants are now going to look at the fourth competency.

 DISPLAY the overhead and *DISTRIBUTE* the handout, *Quality Communication (p. 279)*. Explain that in the next exercise they will practice quality communication and receive feedback on their performance.

LEARNING ACTIVITY

01:15   **Practicing Quality Communication**

 DISTRIBUTE the handout, *Practicing Quality Communication* (p. 178) and *REVIEW* the exercise and its objectives.

 ASSIGN breakout rooms, if used, and assign time to complete the exercise and return to general session.

 DISPLAY the overhead, *The Model for Superior Facilitation* (p. 276).

REMIND participants that they are learning the six competencies required for superior facilitation. They are working on the third competency, *Modeling and Using Quality Communication.*

 DISTRIBUTE and *REVIEW* the *Observation Sheet (Quality Communication)* (p. 181) to be used by the Observer/Timer for this exercise so that everyone understands what is being observed.

00:05   **Debrief**

 REVIEW each example brought back to the general session by the teams and discuss the reasons for the example of poor communication, i.e., was not balanced, or concrete, or respectful, or relevant. (p. 276).

00:10   **Break**

INTERACTIVE PRESENTATION

00:10   **The 5th Competency,**
Understanding and Using the Special Functions of Facilitation

 DISPLAY the overhead, *Special Functions of Facilitation* (p. 281) and review each of the special functions briefly. Full information on the functions is in Chapter 2.

 There is not enough time in a two-day program to practice each of these functions. Any of the functions can be made the topic of a follow-up program. Trainers can also use information on the functions as handouts for participants.

LEARNING ACTIVITY

01:00   **Understanding and Practicing the Special Functions of Facilitation**

 DISTRIBUTE the handout, *Understanding and Practicing the Special Functions of Facilitation* (p. 183) and *REVIEW* the exercise and its objectives.

 ASSIGN breakout rooms, if used, and assign time to complete exercise and return to general session.

 DISTRIBUTE copies of *The Model for Superior Facilitation* (p. 276) and remind participants that they are learning the six competencies required for superior facilitation.

DISTRIBUTE copies of *Special Facilitation Functions* (p. 281) and review the meaning of each of the functions.

 DISTRIBUTE and *REVIEW* the *Observation Sheet (Special Function)* (p. 190) to be used by the Observer/Timer for this exercise so that everyone understands what is being observed.

00:10   **Debrief**

 REVIEW and discuss each of the three key learnings brought back to the general session from the exercise.

00:45   **Lunch**

00:05   **Transition to the 6th Competency:**
                       Understanding and Using Rational Tools

 DISPLAY the overhead, *The Model for Superior Facilitation* (p. 276).

 SHOW participants that they have covered the first five competencies and are now going to practice the sixth competency.

 DISPLAY the overhead, *Types of Rational Tools* (p. 282).

 INTRODUCE the kinds of rational tools that facilitators must master. Indicate that they will practice using tools to develop information and ideas and receive feedback on their performance.

LEARNING ACTIVITY

01:00   **Understanding and Practicing Rational Tools**
                       (Developing Information and Ideas)

 DISTRIBUTE the handout, *Understanding and Practicing Rational Tools (Developing Information and Ideas)* (p. 194) and *REVIEW* the exercise and its objectives.

 ASSIGN breakout rooms, if used, and assign time to complete the exercise and return to general session.

 DISPLAY the overhead, *The Model for Superior Facilitation* (p. 276).

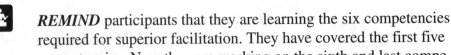

REMIND participants that they are learning the six competencies required for superior facilitation. They have covered the first five competencies. Now they are working on the sixth and last competency, *Understanding and Using Rational Tools.*

DISTRIBUTE copies of *Types of Rational Tools* (p. 282) and review the three kinds of tools. Emphasize that they will be working on the first kind of tool, ones for *Developing Information and Ideas.*

DISPLAY the overhead *DISTRIBUTE* copies of *Tools for Generating Information and Ideas* (p. 283) and review these tools.

DISTRIBUTE and *REVIEW* the *Observation Sheet (Developing Information and Ideas)* (p. 197) to be used by team members in this exercise so that everyone understands what is being observed.

00:10   **Debrief**

Each team will bring back to the general session questions about the tools that they have practiced using. They also will bring back information about how they might use the tool.

REVIEW and respond to questions and review possible uses of the tool.(p. 276).

00:10   **Break**

01:00   **Practicing Facilitation, Putting It All Together**

DISTRIBUTE the handout, *Practicing Facilitation, Putting It All Together* (p. 211) and *REVIEW* the exercise and its objectives.

ASSIGN breakout rooms, if used, and assign time to complete the exercise and return to general session.

DISPLAY the overhead, *The Model for Superior Facilitation* (p. 276).

TELL participants that they will now have the chance to practice all of the skills for superior facilitation.

DISTRIBUTE and *REVIEW* the *Observation Sheet (Putting It All Together)* (p. 214) to be used in this exercise so that participants understand the specific feedback they are to give each other.

00:10   **Debrief**

 Each team will bring back three key learning points from the exercise.

 REVIEW and discuss each team's key learning points.

GROUP ACTIVITY

00:20   **Review and Action Team Activity: Review and Action Logs**

 INSTRUCT Review and Action Teams to use this time to review their key learnings during the program. Ask them to:

- Refer to their first *Review and Action Logs* that they completed at the end of day one.

- Complete their logs for day two.

- Discuss their logs.

If participants are from the same organization, encourage them to commit to a follow-up meeting at a later date to reinforce their learning and support each other's work at becoming superior facilitators.

00:15   **Program Review and Wrap-Up**

 DISTRIBUTE copies of *Objectives for Two-Day Program* (p. 271) and review the objectives.

 DISPLAY the overheads, *The Model for Superior Facilitation* (p. 276) and *Objectives for Two-Day Program* (p. 271). Other overheads you may wish to review include:

- *The Meaning of Superior Facilitation* (p. 277).

- *The Model for Successful Meetings* (p. 278).

- *Quality Communication* (p. 279).

- *Developing Understanding* (p. 280).

- *Special Functions of Facilitation* (p. 281).

- *Types of Rational Tools* (p. 282).

- *Tools for Generating Information and Ideas* (p. 283).

- *Review and Action Teams* (p. 286).

00:15   **Program Evaluation**

 DISTRIBUTE copies of the *Program Evaluation: Long Form* (p. 224). Be sure that you have made copies for each participant.

Chapter Eight

Learning Activities

There are three kinds of learning activities in this chapter:

- Exercises
- Learning Transfer Tools
- Program Evaluation Tools

USING THE LEARNING ACTIVITIES

You may use the learning activities in two ways :

- Key them into your word processing system "as is" or customize them to suit your specific needs .
- Photocopy the learning activities that you need from this book and use them "as is."

The location of each of the learning activities used in the facilitation training designs has been identified in Chapters 4 to 7. However, there are more exercises and learning transfer tools included in this chapter than are specified in the designs in Chapters 4 to 7. Our intention has been to give trainers a resource that meets all of their needs in delivering facilitation training. These additional exercises and tools can be used to customize individual programs or expand existing programs.

Exercises

The exercises you will find in this section have been organized in the following ways:

1. The exercises will generally be in the same sequence that they are used in a facilitation training program. In other words, the exercises early in this section will be the ones that you will be most likely to use in the early part of a program and the later ones will be those that you will typically use in the later part of a program.

2. All the exercises are based on *The Model for Superior Facilitation* found in Chapter 2.

3. All the exercises follow the same format:

    *   Each exercise is designed as a participant handout or as a page in a participant's notebook that you might put together for your facilitation training program.

    *   A place is given for you to insert the time that participants have for completing the exercise. We have recommended times listed for each exercise. But times will necessarily change with the number of participants in a program, the number of participants cooperating (working as teams) on an exercise, and your own style.

    *   Each exercise has a set of objectives that describe what outcomes are expected from the exercise.

    *   Following the stated objectives, each exercise lists the tasks that participants are expected to perform and the order in which they are to be performed.

4. Each exercise has two parts. The first part is a page of *Trainer's Notes*. The second part is the *Handout* for each participant. We have given you a short set of instructions for setting up each exercise and debriefing each exercise in the *Program Flow* section of each design described in Chapters 4 to 7. We did this to give you a good idea of the content of each design and to give you a tool for general planning. The *Trainer's Notes* that precede each exercise are more detailed. You will find that these notes will provide you with considerable assistance until you have repeated the exercises several times and become thoroughly familiar with them.

<u>TRAINER'S NOTES</u>	## Clarifying the Model for Superior Facilitation
Objectives	To ensure that participants understand *The Model for Superior Facilitation* and its relationship to the practice of facilitating meetings, can relate the model to the definition of superior facilitation, and have a working knowledge of the six competencies for superior facilitation.
Description	This exercise begins the process of establishing superior facilitation as a cognitive activity, based on a concrete *understanding* of what superior facilitation involves. The exercise follows an interactive presentation by the trainer that outlines the information contained in the model, the meaning of the elements in the model, and their relationship to each other. The exercise lays the foundation for all subsequent learning activities in the training program.
Time	25 minutes
Resources	Provide copies of the following for each participant:

- *Clarifying the Model for Superior Facilitation* (p. 124)
- *The Model for Superior Facilitation* (p. 276)

Presentation

1. Review the exercise and its objectives, keeping the overhead of *The Model for Superior Facilitation* on the screen during the exercise.

2. Assign breakout rooms, if used, and assign time to complete the exercise and return to general session.

3. Remind participants that they will be using the model in all future activities in the program.

Debrief   Make sure the following ideas are brought out:

- Superior facilitation is any useful thing that any team member does or any designated facilitator does that helps a team have a successful meeting.

- Superior facilitation is based on the six competencies. Review each of the six competencies, using *The Model for Superior Facilitation*.

<u>HANDOUT</u>

Clarifying the Model for Superior Facilitation

You have _____ minutes for this exercise.

Objectives

To ensure that participants understand *The Model for Superior Facilitation* and its relationship to the practice of facilitating meetings. Participants should be able to relate the model to the definition of *Superior Facilitation* and have a working knowledge of the six competencies for superior facilitation.

Directions

1. Review this exercise as a team and ensure that your team understands what tasks it must complete.

2. Each person works independently and spends a few moments reviewing *The Model for Superior Facilitation*. Note any questions that you have about the model, its elements, and how they are related.

3. Have one team member volunteer to give his/her *understanding* of the model and how it describes superior facilitation. After this person has finished, go around to each remaining member and have that member add anything that he/she feels might help further clarify the model.

4. Review any questions that members noted about the model in task #2 and task #3. Have a team member record any questions about the model that the team would like to have discussed in the general session. Bring these questions to the general session.

Understanding the Meaning of Superior Facilitation

Objectives

To ensure that participants understand the meaning of superior facilitation that will be used throughout the program and the distinction between facilitator and facilitation.

Description

This exercise begins the process of ensuring that participants have a clear and concrete *understanding* of each of the six competencies identified in *The Model for Superior Facilitation*. In this exercise they compare the meaning of superior facilitation with the understandings of facilitation that they have as they begin the training program. The purpose is to highlight just how superior facilitation differs from most other definitions because it relates facilitation to *results*. Also, this exercise helps participants make the useful distinction between facilitation and facilitator.

Time

25 minutes

Resources

Provide copies of the following for each participant:

- *Understanding the Meaning of Superior Facilitation* (p. 126)

- *The Meaning of Superior Facilitation* (p. 277)

Presentation

1. Review the exercise and its objectives.

2. Assign breakout rooms, if used, and assign time to complete the exercise and return to general session.

3. Remind participants that the definition of superior facilitation is the basis for what will be emphasized in the program, and it is the definition which is a major guide to their learning how to become superior facilitators.

4. Use the overhead, *The Meaning of Superior Facilitation* (p.277), to convey the meaning of superior facilitation as the first of the six competencies for superior facilitation.

Debrief

Make sure the following ideas are brought out:

- Superior facilitation is based on *The Model for Superior Facilitation*, identifying six competencies of superior facilitation.

- The first competency is *Understanding the Meaning of Superior Facilitation*.

- The meaning of superior facilitation emphasizes facilitation that produces *results*.

- Emphasize the distinction between facilitator and facilitation (i.e., anyone who makes useful input facilitates, whether he/she is a designated facilitator or not) using the following overheads:

  - *The Meaning of Superior Facilitation* (p. 277)

  - *The Model for Superior Facilitation* (p. 276)

<u>H</u>ANDOUT   **Understanding the Meaning of Superior Facilitation**

You have _____ minutes for this exercise.

Objectives   To ensure that participants are clear about the meaning of superior facilitation that will be used throughout the program and understand the distinction between facilitator and facilitation.

Directions   1. Review this exercise as a team (your table is your team) and ensure that your team understands what tasks it must complete.

2. Each person works independently and spends a few moments reviewing the definition of facilitation found below. Note any questions that you have about the definition.

SUPERIOR FACILITATION

Superior facilitation consists of inputs (actions) by one or more persons that help teams **achieve** their goals and **maintain** or **improve** their competencies to achieve their goals.

---

3. Have one team member volunteer to give his/her *understanding* of the definition and how it might differ from his/her current *understanding* of the meaning of facilitation. After this person has finished, go around to each remaining member and have that member repeat the process begun by the first member.

4. Appoint a person to record the *results* of this task. Discuss how the definition of facilitation that will be used in the program differs (if it does) from what members of the team might understand facilitation to mean.

5. Review any questions that members noted about the model in task #3 and task #4. Have the recorder bring these questions to the general session.

Blocks to Successful Meetings

Objectives

To further participants' *understanding* of the major behaviors and conditions that block successful meetings and to develop common information for *understanding The Model for Successful Meetings.*

Description

This exercise begins to prepare participants for *The Model for Successful Meetings* which will be developed later. Everyone has a good idea about the reasons that meetings don't work very well. This exercise uses the experiences of participants to develop the elements in *The Model for Successful Meetings*. It is expected that one major learning from the exercise is that the most general reason that meetings fail is that people do not have or use a model of a successful meeting.

Time

25 minutes

Resources

Provide copies of the following for each participant:

- *Blocks to Successful Meetings* (p. 128)
- *The Model for Successful Meetings* (p. 278)

Presentation

1. Review the exercise and its objectives.

2. Assign breakout rooms, if used, and assign time to complete the exercise and return to general session.

3. Remind participants that they are in the process of examining each of the six competencies identified in *The Model for Superior Facilitation.*

4. Remind participants that having in their minds just what a good meeting looks like is essential for superior facilitation and that you are going to develop such a model, using their own experience.

Debrief

The trainer firsts makes an interactive presentation to describe *The Model for Successful Meetings.* After the model has been presented, the trainer has each team present the *results* of the exercise. The trainer uses the information presented and (with the help of the group) assigns each item to one of the elements or subelements in the model. Using the overhead, *The Model for Successful Meetings* (p. 278), make sure the following ideas are brought out:

- Superior facilitation depends on our having a clear picture in our minds of what a successful meeting looks like.

- We already know from our own experience the kinds of things that block successful meetings.

- A successful meeting is created by avoiding these blocks.

<u>HANDOUT</u>

Blocks to Successful Meetings

You have _____ minutes for this exercise.

Objectives

To further our *understanding* of the major behaviors and conditions that block successful meetings and to develop common information for better *understanding The Model for Successful Meetings* which we will be developing.

Directions

1. Review this exercise as a team and ensure that your team understands what tasks it must complete.

2. Select a recorder who will collect the information developed by your team and report it in the general session.

3. Each team member takes five minutes to think about a small group meeting in which he/she participated which was not as successful as it might have been. Each team member jots down the reasons or blocks that kept the meeting from being fully successful and the people involved from doing their best.

4. Use a round-robin method (going from one team member to the next for a single block until all blocks are listed) and develop a list of the blocks that your team members have experienced during meetings. You do not have to reach a consensus, just list all the different blocks that you can.

5. Select six of the most common blocks that best represent the common experiences of your team members. Bring these to the general session for discussion.

Clarifying the Model for Successful Meetings

Objectives

To ensure that each team member has a clear *understanding* of the key elements in *The Model for Successful Meetings*, of how the key elements are interrelated, and that each team member can determine what questions need to be answered related to the meaning and use of the model.

Description

This exercise ensures that participants have a solid *understanding* of *The Model for Successful Meetings*. The model forms a framework that participants can use in learning to facilitate meetings. The model equips participants with a set of categories which they can use to classify the kinds of problems that they will observe during a meeting and helps them decide just what kind of input to make to facilitate the progress of a meeting.

Time

20 minutes

Resources

Provide copies of the following for each participant:

- *Clarifying the Model for Successful Meetings* (p. 130)

- *The Model for Successful Meetings* (p. 278)

Presentation

1. Review the exercise and its objectives, keeping the overhead of *The Model for Successful Meetings* (p. 278) on screen during the exercise.

2. Assign breakout rooms, if used, and assign time to complete exercise and return to general session.

3. Remind participants that *understanding* and using the model is the second of the six competencies used in superior facilitation.

Debrief

Have each team present its questions. Using a round-robin method, take a question from one table, a second from the next, and so on until all questions have been presented. As each question is presented, involve the whole group in answering. Then, review each of the elements and subelements in *The Model for Successful Meetings*.

<u>H</u>ANDOUT

Clarifying the Model for Successful Meetings

You have _____ minutes for this exercise.

Objectives

To ensure that each team member has a clear *understanding* of the key elements in *The Model for Successful Meetings*, that each team member understands how the key elements are interrelated, and to determine what questions need to be answered related to the meaning and use of the model.

Directions

1. Review this exercise as a team and ensure that your team understands what tasks it must complete.

2. Each team member takes ten minutes to review *The Model for Successful Meetings* and to jot down any questions that he/she has about the meaning and use of the model.

3. Review as a team each of the following elements: *resources*, *structure*, and *results*. For each element discuss the following:

   • Its meaning.

   • How it relates to each of the other elements or influences these elements.

   • What problems would you expect when an element is not managed properly?

4. Review your questions from task #2. Have your questions been answered? Are there additional questions about the model that your team would like to have answered?

5. Bring any questions that you have about the model to the general session.

TRAINER'S NOTES

Clarifying Potential
and Its Subelement, Structure

Objectives   To ensure that each team member has a clear *understanding* of *potential* and its subelement, *structure*, and that each team member can describe behaviors that occur during a meeting that suggest that the team needs to strengthen its *structure*.

Description   This exercise continues the process of ensuring that participants fully understand *The Model for Successful Meetings* and are beginning to develop skills in using the model to diagnose problems. In this exercise they identify as many behaviors as they can which might suggest that a team has not properly structured itself to have a superior meeting.

Time   25 minutes

Resources   Provide copies of the following for each participant:

- *Clarifying Potential and Its Subelement, Structure* (p. 132)

- *The Model for Successful Meetings* (p. 278)

Presentation   1. Review the exercise and its objectives.

2. Assign breakout rooms, if used, and assign time to complete the exercise and return to general session.

3. Put the overhead of *The Model for Superior Facilitation* (p. 276) on the screen. Remind participants that they are learning the six competencies required for superior facilitation. The second competency is *Understanding and Using the Model for Successful Meetings*. They have had an overview of *The Model for Successful Meetings*. Now they will begin to look at each of the elements and subelements in greater detail.

Debrief   Have each team put its chart up so that each chart is visible to all members of the training group. Starting with the first behavior listed, identify with the group behaviors from other charts that are essentially the same. Discuss why the behavior suggests a problem in *structure*. Repeat the process until all items are covered. Discuss any questions that the teams identified related to *structure*.

<u>**HANDOUT**</u>

Clarifying Potential and Its Subelement, Structure

You have _____ minutes for this exercise.

Objectives

To ensure that each team member has a clear *understanding* of *potential* and its subelement, *structure,* and can describe behaviors that occur during a meeting that suggest that the team needs to strengthen its *structure.*

Directions

1. Review this exercise as a team and ensure that your team understands what tasks it must complete.

2. Each team member takes five minutes to review the description of *potential* and *structure* found below. *Structure* is the first subelement in *potential.* As you read, jot down any questions that you have.

POTENTIAL AND ITS SUBELEMENT, STRUCTURE

A meeting starts with a certain level of potential. This is the first element. A meeting may have a high or low potential for achieving success. The higher the potential, the more likely it is that a high level of success will be achieved. A team, for example, that is composed of people who do not have the knowledge or skill to perform an assigned task, has low potential. A team composed of people who do not know how to work together has a low potential. The potential of a team **results** from two subelements: structure and **resources**.

Building structure can be thought of as helping a team do whatever it must do to proceed in an efficient and effective manner toward its goals. When we help a team manage its structure, we are helping it take full advantage of its **resources**. When we facilitate the development of structure we are helping a team become explicit and conscious about such things as norms, roles, goals, and processes.

NORMS

These are the rules and values that the team makes explicit about the way it will conduct its business during a meeting. Norms include such items as:

- Determining that a meeting will start and end on time.
- How each member will be assured of being heard.
- How conflict will be resolved.
- What is expected of each member.

ROLES

Another way a team structures itself for a successful meeting is by making explicit what roles members will occupy and how people are expected to perform in these roles. Making information about roles explicit includes:

- Determining if a meeting will have a designated leader and what the job of the leader will be.
- Determining if there will be a facilitator and what the functions of the facilitator will be.
- Determining what other roles must be clarified, e.g., if the supervisor or manager of the group is present, how will he/she function in the team.

3. Review as a team the meaning of *structure*. Discuss any questions that members have about facilitators helping teams manage their *structure*. Record any questions that you wish to bring to the general session.

4. Put "Structure" at the top of a piece of chart paper. Work as a team and list as many behaviors as you can that you might observe during a meeting that would suggest that the team needs to do something to manage its *structure*, i.e., improve or strengthen them. Refine your list and bring it to the general session for discussion.

Clarifying Potential and Its Subelement, Resources

Objectives

To ensure that each team member has a clear *understanding* of *potential* and its second subelement, *resources,* and that each team member can describe behaviors that occur during a meeting that suggest that the team needs to strengthen or manage its *resources* better.

Description

This exercise continues the process of ensuring that participants fully understand *The Model for Successful Meetings* and begin to develop skills in using the model to diagnose problems. In this exercise they identify as many behaviors as they can which might suggest that a team is having a problem identifying or using the *resources* necessary to perform its tasks.

Time

25 minutes

Resources

Provide copies of the following for each participant:

- *Clarifying Potential and Its Subelement, Resources* (p. 135)

- *The Model for Successful Meetings* (p. 278)

Presentation

1. Review the exercise and its objectives, keeping the overhead of *The Model for Successful Meetings* on screen during the exercise. In this exercise the subject is *potential* and its subelement, *resources.*

2. Assign breakout rooms, if used, and assign time to complete the exercise and return to general session.

3. Remind participants that *understanding* and using the model is the second of the six competencies used in superior facilitation.

Debrief

Have each team put its chart up so that each chart is visible to all members of the training group. Starting with the first behavior listed, identify with the group behaviors from other charts that are essentially the same. Discuss why the behavior suggests a problem in *resources.* Repeat the process until all items are covered. Discuss any questions that the teams identified related to *resources.*

<u>HANDOUT</u>	## Clarifying Potential and Its Subelement, Resources

You have _____ minutes for this exercise.

Objectives

To ensure that each team member has a clear *understanding* of *potential* and its second subelement, *resources,* and can describe behaviors that occur during a meeting that suggest that the team needs to strengthen or manage better its *resources*.

Directions

1. Review this exercise as a team and ensure that your team understands what tasks it must complete.

2. Each team member takes five minutes to review the following description of *potential* and its subelement, *resources*. As you read, jot down any questions that you have.

3. Review as a team the meaning of *resources*. Discuss any questions that members have about facilitators helping teams manage their *resources*. Record any questions that you wish to bring to the general session.

4. Put "Resources" at the top of a piece of chart paper. Work as a team to list as many behaviors as you can that you might observe during a meeting that would suggest that the team needs to do something to manage its *resources*, i.e., improve or strengthen them. Refine your list and bring it to the general session for discussion.

POTENTIAL AND ITS SUBELEMENT, RESOURCES

A meeting starts with a certain level of potential. This is the first element. A meeting may have a high or low potential for achieving success. The higher the potential, the more likely it is that a high level of success will be achieved. A team, for example, that is composed of people who do not have the knowledge or skill to perform an assigned task, has low potential. A team composed of people who do not know how to work together has a low potential. The potential of a team **results** from two subelements: **structure** and **resources**.

RESOURCES

Resources refer to all the human, informational, environmental, technical, and material supports and means required for a team to do its best job during a meeting. **Resources** are strengthened by:

- Having the right people with the appropriate knowledge, skills, and experience.
- Having people at the meeting who are committed to the purposes of the meeting.
- Ensuring that people at the meeting have done their homework and are prepared for the meeting.
- Ensuring that relevant information is available to people attending the meeting.
- Ensuring that there is an adequate meeting room.
- Ensuring that equipment like projectors, flipcharts, and recorders are present—if they are needed.
- Ensuring that the time given for the meeting is appropriate to the tasks of the meeting.
- Ensuring members are skilled in communication and problem solving.

Notes

- _____
- _____
- _____
- _____
- _____
- _____
- _____
- _____
- _____
- _____
- _____
- _____
- _____

<u>TRAINER'S NOTES</u>

Clarifying Performance and Its Subelement, Quality Communication

Objectives

To ensure that each team member has a clear *understanding* of *performance* and its first subelement, *quality communication,* and can describe behaviors that occur during a meeting that suggest the team needs to strengthen or better manage its communication.

Description

This exercise continues the process of ensuring that participants fully understand *The Model for Successful Meetings* and begin to develop skills in using the model to diagnose problems. In this exercise they identify as many behaviors as they can which might suggest that team members are not using quality communication in their interactions and discussions.

Time

25 minutes

Resources

Provide copies of the following for each participant:

- *Clarifying Performance and Its Subelement, Quality Communication* (p. 138)

- *The Model for Successful Meetings* (p. 278)

- *Quality Communication* (p. 279)

Presentation

1. Review the exercise and its objectives, keeping the overhead of *The Model for Successful Meetings* on the screen as you set up this exercise.

2. Assign breakout rooms, if used, and assign time to complete the exercise and return to general session.

3. Remind participants that they have gained a general *understanding* of the model and have looked in detail at the first element in the model, *potential.* The second element in the model is *performance.* This is the subject of this exercise and the ones to follow.

4. Review the meaning of *performance* and its subelements.

5. Display the overhead *Quality Communication* (p. 279) and review characteristics of quality communication.

Debrief

Have each team put its chart up so that the chart is visible to all members of the training group. Starting with the first behavior listed, identify with the group behaviors from other charts that are essentially the same. Discuss why the behavior suggests a problem in communication. Repeat the process until all items are covered. Discuss any questions that the teams identified related to quality communication.

<u>**Handout**</u>

Clarifying Performance and Its Subelement, Quality Communication

You have _____ minutes for this exercise.

Objectives

To ensure that each team member has a clear *understanding* of *performance* and its first subelement, *quality communication,* and can describe behaviors that occur during a meeting that suggest that the team needs to strengthen or better manage its quality communication.

Directions

1. Review this exercise as a team and ensure that your team understands what tasks it must complete.

2. Each team member takes five minutes to review the description of *performance* and its subelement, *quality communication*, found below. As you read, jot down any questions you have.

PERFORMANCE AND ITS SUBELEMENT, QUALITY COMMUNICATION

The first element that facilitators must help teams manage is their potential. The second element is the way the team actually performs during its meeting, i.e., how people interact and communicate. **Performance** builds on the team's potential.

There are three subelements in a team's interaction that must be managed and maintained at the highest level in order to produce the highest results from a meeting. These subelements are:

- Use of quality communication.
- Consistent development of understanding in each member of the team.
- Use of rational processes.

The facilitator's job is to help teams use quality communication, develop a thorough understanding on the part of members about what is happening during a meeting, and help the team use appropriate rational processes.

QUALITY COMMUNICATION

Quality communication supports the **performance** of a team. Whenever communication is irrelevant, untimely, vague, disrespectful, or centered on individual needs rather than team needs, it fails to further the purposes of the team. Facilitators must, of course, model quality communication. They must also help members use quality communication during their meetings.

Quality communication furthers the purposes of the team meeting because it is:

Interactive and Balanced	Everyone is involved, no one dominates.
Concrete	What is communicated is concrete and easily understood.
Respectful	What is communicated does not target the mistakes, errors, weaknesses of members, but focuses on issues, problems, data, goals, and the like.
Relevant	It supports what the team is doing and the team's process for doing it, i.e., content and process.

3. Review as a team the meaning of *performance* and its first subelement, *quality communication*. Discuss any questions that members have about facilitators helping teams manage their communication. Record any questions that you wish to bring to the general session.

4. Put "Quality Communication" at the top of a piece of chart paper. Work as a team to list as many behaviors as you can that you might observe during a meeting that would suggest that the team needs to do something to manage its communication, i.e., improve or strengthen it. Refine your list and bring it to the general session for discussion.

TRAINER'S NOTES

Clarifying Performance and Its Subelement, Understanding

Objectives

To ensure that each team member has a clear *understanding* of *performance* and its second subelement, *understanding,* and can describe behaviors that occur during a meeting that suggest that the team needs to strengthen or better manage its *understanding*.

Description

This exercise continues the process of ensuring that participants fully understand *The Model for Successful Meetings* and begin to develop skills in using the model to diagnose problems. In this exercise they identify as many behaviors as they can which suggest that team members do not fully understand what the team is doing or the specific topic being discussed.

Time

25 minutes

Resources

Provide copies of the following for each participant:

- *Clarifying Performance and Its Subelement, Understanding* (p. 141)

- *The Model for Successful Meetings* (p. 278)

Presentation

1. Review the exercise and its objectives, keeping the overhead of *The Model for Successful Meetings* (p. 278) on the screen as you set up the exercise.

2. Assign breakout rooms, if used, and assign time to complete the exercise and return to general session.

3. Remind participants that they are looking at the second element in the model, *performance*. We have looked at the first subelement in *performance, quality communication.* The second subelement is *understanding*.

Debrief

Have each team put its chart up so that each chart is visible to all members of the team. Starting with the first behavior listed, identify with the team behaviors from other charts that are essentially the same. Discuss why the behavior suggests a problem in developing *understanding* among team members of what is being discussed or about what the team is trying to do. Repeat the process until all items are covered. Discuss any questions that the teams identified related to behaviors which relate to poor *understanding*.

<u>HANDOUT</u>

Clarifying Performance and Its Subelement, Understanding

You have _____ minutes for this exercise.

Objectives

To ensure that each team member has a clear *understanding* of *performance* and its second subelement, *understanding,* and can describe behaviors that occur during a meeting that suggest that the team needs to strengthen or better manage its *understanding*.

Directions

1. Review this exercise as a team and ensure that your team understands what tasks it must complete.

2. Each team member takes five minutes to review the description of *performance* and its subelement, *understanding*. As you read, jot down any questions that you have.

3. Review as a team and discuss any questions that members have regarding facilitators helping teams to develop understanding among members about what the team is doing at all times. Record any questions that you wish to bring to the general session.

4. Put "Understanding" at the top of a piece of chart paper. Work as a team and list as many behaviors as you can that you might observe during a meeting that would suggest that members of the team do not understand each other, or do not understand certain facts, or may not be making certain important connections. Refine your list and bring it to the general session for discussion.

PERFORMANCE AND ITS SUBELEMENT, UNDERSTANDING

The first element that facilitators must help teams manage is their potential. The second element is the way the team actually performs during its meeting, i.e., how people interact and communicate. **Performance** builds on the team's potential. There are three subelements in **performance**, quality communication, developing **understanding**, and using rational tools.

Understanding is created through the give and take of members interacting with each other. **Understanding** typically requires that information be clarified or summarized. **Understanding** is also created by making connections and showing the relationships that exist among the information and ideas produced during a meeting. A major job of facilitators is to ensure that all members at a meeting understand what is going on at all times.

THEY SUMMARIZE

They also further **understanding** by having input periodically summarized. Facilitators may summarize for the team what has been communicated, or what has been decided, or what action is planned. Whenever possible, however, the facilitator should encourage team members to make their own summaries.

4.

THEY CLARIFY

They clarify what is being communicated and clarify what the team is doing. One way to clarify what is being communicated is to rephrase inputs or request members to rephrase what they think another member has said. Another way that facilitators clarify is by helping members become as concrete as possible in what they are communicating. Often this means something as simple as suggesting that members give examples of what they are saying.

THEY REMIND

Facilitators not only clarify what is being communicated, they also clarify for the team what it is doing by keeping the team conscious. This means reminding the team what it has set out to do, letting the team know when it has gotten side tracked, helping the team stick to the steps or rules of the rational tool it may be using.

THEY MAKE CONNECTIONS

Facilitators further **understanding** by helping a team make connections. Inputs from facilitators that help a team make connections might sound like the following: "In the light of your deciding to do A, how will that affect your earlier decision to do B?" "Do any of the causes for the problem that you have identified share anything in common?" "Do any of these strategies seem to be at odds with each other—are they all fully compatible with each other?"

TRAINER'S NOTES   # Clarifying Performance and Its Subelement, Rational Tools

Objectives

To ensure that each team member has a clear understanding of *performance* and its third subelement, *rational tools,* and can describe behaviors that occur during a meeting that suggest that the team needs to strengthen or better manage its rational tools.

Description

This exercise continues the process of ensuring that participants fully understand *The Model for Successful Meetings* and begin to develop skills in using the model to diagnose problems. In this exercise they identify as many behaviors as they can which might suggest that team members are not making good use of various rational tools to help them do their job.

Time

25 minutes

Resources

Provide copies of the following for each participant:

- *Clarifying Performance and Its Subelement, Rational Tools* (p. 144)

- *The Model for Successful Meetings* (p. 278)

Presentation

1. Review the exercise and its objectives, keeping the overhead of *The Model for Successful Meetings* (p. 278) on the screen as you set up the exercise.

2. Assign breakout rooms, if used, and assign time to complete the exercise and return to general session.

3. Remind participants that they are looking at the second element in the model, *performance.* You have gained an understanding in detail of the first element in the model, *potential.* The second element in the model is *performance.* The first subelement in *performance* that we looked at was *quality communication,* the second subelement was *developing understanding,* and the third subelement is using *rational tools.*

Debrief

Have each team put its chart up so that each chart is visible to all members of the training group. Starting with the first behavior listed, identify with the group behaviors from other charts that are essentially the same. Discuss why the behavior suggests a problem in using rational tools. Repeat the process until all items are covered. Then, discuss any questions that the teams identified related to rational tools.

<u>H</u>ANDOUT

Clarifying Performance and Its Subelement, Rational Tools

You have _____ minutes for this exercise.

Objectives

To ensure that each team member has a clear understanding of *performance* and its third subelement, *rational tools,* and can describe behaviors that occur during a meeting that suggest that the team needs to strengthen or better manage its rational tools.

Directions

1. Review this exercise as a team and ensure that your team understands what tasks it must complete.

2. Each team member takes five minutes to review the description of *performance* and its subelement, *rational tools*, found below. As you read, jot down any questions that you have.

3. Review as a team the meaning of *performance* and its third subelement, *rational tools*. Discuss any questions that members have about facilitators helping teams manage their communication. Record any questions that you wish to bring to the general session.

4. Put "Rational Tools" at the top of a piece of chart paper. Work as a team and list as many behaviors as you can that you might observe during a meeting that would suggest that the team needs to do something to manage how it is using its rational tools. Refine your list and bring it to the general session for discussion.

PERFORMANCE AND ITS SUBELEMENT, RATIONAL TOOLS

The first element that facilitators must help teams manage is their potential. The second element is the way the team actually performs during its meeting, i.e., how people interact and communicate. **Performance** builds on the team's potential.

RATIONAL TOOLS

Rational tools refer to any structured sequence of steps that help a team develop information or solve problems. A rational tool may establish the structure of an entire meeting or series of meetings by identifying each step that a team has set out to follow as it conducts its business. A rational tool may be as specific and finite as brainstorming, cause-and-effect diagrams, or the nominal group technique. A rational tool may be as general as establishing the sequence for a discussion or the steps in solving a problem.

The facilitator's job is to help the team identify and use appropriate rational tools, to stay conscious of what they are doing as they use the tool, and to stick with the steps and procedures included in the tool.

Rational tools are, of course, closely related to structure. We have included them as a part of **performance** to emphasize that it is not just deciding to use a tool that is useful, but sticking to the steps or process defined in the tool that is required. Deciding to use a rational tool is the first step (structuring). Using the tool is the next step (**performance**).

<table>
<tr>
<td>

TRAINER'S NOTES

</td>
<td>

Clarifying Results and Its Subelements, Achievement of Goals and Improvement of Team Competencies

</td>
</tr>
<tr>
<td>

Objectives

</td>
<td>

To ensure that each team member has a clear understanding of *results* and its two subelements, *achievement of goals* and *improvement of team competencies,* and can describe behaviors that occur during a meeting that suggest that the team needs to strengthen or manage better its *results.*

</td>
</tr>
<tr>
<td>

Description

</td>
<td>

This exercise continues the process of ensuring that participants fully understand each element in *The Model for Successful Meetings*. This exercise covers the last element, *results*. In this exercise they do the following:

- Review the meaning of *results* in *The Model for Successful Meetings*.

- Identify as many behaviors as they can which might suggest that teams are not achieving good task *results.*

- Identify actions that teams might take to strengthen their competencies to improve future meetings.

</td>
</tr>
<tr>
<td>

Time

</td>
<td>

25 minutes

</td>
</tr>
<tr>
<td>

Resources

</td>
<td>

Provide copies of the following for each participant:

- *Clarifying Results and Its Subelements, Achievement of Goals and Improvement of Team Competencies* (p. 148)

- *The Model for Successful Meetings* (p. 278)

</td>
</tr>
<tr>
<td>

Presentation

</td>
<td>

1. Review the exercise and its objectives, keeping the overhead of *The Model for Successful Meetings* (p. 278) on the screen as you set up the exercise.

2. Assign breakout rooms, if used, and assign time to complete the exercise and return to general session.

3. Using *The Model for Successful Meetings*, remind participants that they have gained a general understanding of the model and its first two elements, *potential* and *performance*. The last element in the model is *results*. *Results* has two subelements, *Achievement of Goals* and *Strengthening Team Competencies.*

</td>
</tr>
</table>

Debrief

Each team will have two charts, one that lists behaviors related to goal achievement and the second that lists actions that teams might take to maintain or strengthen their competency for improving future meetings.

Have each team put its first chart up, "Goal Achievement," so that each chart is visible to all members of the training group. Starting with the first behavior listed, identify with the group behaviors from other charts that are essentially the same. Discuss why the behavior suggests a problem in goal achievement. Repeat the process until all items are covered. Repeat the same process and cover behaviors related to "Improving Team Competencies." Discuss any questions that the teams identified related to *results*.

Notes

- _____
- _____
- _____
- _____
- _____
- _____
- _____
- _____
- _____
- _____
- _____
- _____
- _____
- _____
- _____
- _____
- _____
- _____
- _____
- _____

<u>H</u>ANDOUT

Clarifying Results and Its Subelements, Achievement of Goals and Improvement of Team Competencies

You have _____ minutes for this exercise.

Objectives

To ensure that each team member has a clear understanding of *results* and its two subelements, *achievement of goals* and *improved meetings*, and can describe behaviors that occur during a meeting that suggest that the team needs to strengthen or better manage its *results*.

Directions

1. Review this exercise as a team and ensure that your team understands what tasks it must complete.

2. Each team member takes five minutes to review the description of *results* and its subelements found below. As you read, jot down any questions that you have.

RESULTS AND ITS SUBELEMENTS

The first element that facilitators must help teams manage is their potential. The second element is the way the team actually performs during its meeting, i.e., how people interact and communicate. The third element is **results**.

The third and final element in *The Model for Successful Meetings* is **results**. Facilitation consists of inputs given by one or more persons that help teams maximize their potential and maximize the quality of their **performance** (i.e., their interaction and communication) so that they achieve the best possible **results** during a meeting. This definition suggests that there has been no facilitation unless the team has been helped to achieve its goals .

Meetings must be judged by the **results** they produce. A successful team meeting produces two kinds of **results**. The first result is that the meeting achieves the goals that have been set. The second result is that the team learns from its meetings and strengthens its competencies to improve its future meetings.

Subelement #1

ACHIEVEMENT OF GOALS

The immediate purpose of any meeting is to achieve a set of goals or perform a set of tasks. *The Model for Successful Meetings* clearly communicates the idea that the best **results** are achieved by managing the other elements and subel e-ments in the model. **Results** are indirect outcomes. The degree to which teams manage their resources, structure, rational processes, communication, and understanding will determine the quality of the tasks they achieve .

Take the matter of clarity as an example. A team begins to develop clarity by properly managing the way it structures itself, i.e., the way it takes time to make certain the goals, roles, and processes of the team are explicit and understood by everyone. Clarity is also an issue in the **performance** of a team. Over and over again, facilitators will help teams clarify what they are doing and why they are doing it .

The kind of tasks that a team sets out to achieve during a meeting is an open set. There is no limit to the kinds of tasks that teams have. Everything depends on the kind of team that is meeting. Learning teams will have their tasks, problem solving teams will have different tasks, accident investigation teams will have still different tasks, and so on. The tasks change with the kind of team that is meeting. When work teams, process improvement teams, management teams, and other kinds of teams meet, they may have set for themselves the task of developing themselves as teams.

The job of facilitators is not to set the tasks for the team. The job of the facilitator is to help these teams clarify their tasks and achieve these tasks. Clarification starts with the way teams structure themselves and continues throughout their

Subelement #2

STRENGTHEN TEAM COMPETENCIES

A second result of successful team meetings is that members learn from the meeting so that they can improve their future meetings. This result can, of course, only directly apply to teams which meet more than once. It can, however, apply indirectly as individuals learn from any meeting in which they participate so that they can improve any future meetings in which they participate. Competencies can be strengthened by various strategies. Among these are regular evaluation of meetings, structuring performance feedback for each team member, observing the performance of other teams, investigating various information resources about meetings.

The Model for Successful Meetings makes the improvement of meetings an explicit expected result. The model can be used as a tool for evaluating the way a team runs a meeting and help them target opportunities for improvement.

---

3. Review as a team the meaning of *results* and its subelements. Discuss any questions that members have about facilitators helping teams manage their *results*.

4. Managing *results* is largely a matter of managing the other two elements that make up a successful team meeting; *potential* and *performance*. A team meeting is a process, like any other process of production. We can best fix or improve the *results* or outputs from a production process indirectly, that is by managing how the output was produced. Monitoring the quality of output, however, is one important way to discover that we have a problem or that something should be improved.

   Put "Goal Achievement" at the top of a piece of chart paper. Work as a team to list as many indicators as you can that might suggest that the team is not achieving its goals, or that its goals should be modified.

5. Put "Improved Team Competencies" at the top of a piece of chart paper. Work as a team to list specific actions that a team might take to strengthen its competencies for improving its meetings. Give as many concrete examples as you can from your own experiences. Refine your lists from tasks #4 and #5 and bring these to the general session for discussion.

<table>
<tr><td>

Objectives

Description

Time

Resources

Presentation

</td><td>

Practicing Facilitation, Helping the Team Develop Its Potential

To ensure that participants understand the meaning of developing a team's *potential* and provide feedback on their skills that help a team develop its *potential*, i.e., *resources* and *structure*.

This exercise begins to develop actual facilitation skills in participants by having them practice the use of a part of *The Model for Successful Meetings*. Up until now they have been discussing and clarifying *The Model for Successful Meetings*, its elements, and subelements. Participants work in small teams, and each participant takes a turn as designated facilitator. At the end of each practice round, the designated facilitator receives feedback from the other team members concerning his/her demonstrated skills. It is strongly recommended that videotaping and replay be used in this exercise.

You must allow at least twenty minutes for each participant to function as a facilitator, if you use videotaping and replay. Allow fifteen minutes per participant if you do not use video. You must also factor in time to set up the exercise. For a team of five participants, using video, this exercise will take approximately two hours. In the one- and two-day designs we have allowed for three practice rounds and a total time of one hour fifteen minutes for the exercise.

Provide copies of the following for each participant:

- *Practicing Facilitation, Helping the Team Develop Its Potential* (p. 153)
- *Observation Sheet (Potential)* (p. 156)
- *The Model for Successful Meetings* (p. 278)

1. Review the exercise and its objectives.

2. Assign breakout rooms, if used, and assign time to complete the exercise and return to general session.

3. Put the overhead of *The Model for Superior Facilitation* (p. 276) on the screen. Remind participants that they are learning the six competencies required for superior facilitation and are presently working on the second competency, Using *The Model for Successful Meetings*.

4. Keep the overhead of *The Model for Successful Meetings* (p. 278) on screen as you set up this exercise.

5. Emphasize that participants will focus on the first element in the model, *potential*, and practice helping a team develop and use *resources* and *structure*.

6. Go over the *Observation Sheet* and ensure that participants are clear how they will use the sheet in the exercise.

</td></tr>
</table>

151

Debrief

Each team will bring back three key learning points from the exercise. Review each team's key learning points. Conduct a general discussion about *The Model for Successful Meetings* and the function of helping a team develop and use *resources* and *structure*.

Notes

- _____
- _____
- _____
- _____
- _____
- _____
- _____
- _____
- _____
- _____
- _____
- _____
- _____
- _____
- _____
- _____
- _____
- _____
- _____
- _____
- _____
- _____
- _____

<u>**HANDOUT**</u>

**Practicing Facilitation,
Helping the Team Develop Its Potential**

You have _____ minutes for this exercise.

Objectives

To ensure that participants understand the meaning of developing a team's potential and provide feedback on their skills that help a team develop its *potential*, i.e., *resources* and *structure*.

Directions

1. Review this exercise as a team and ensure that your team understands what tasks it must complete.

2. Each team member takes five minutes to review *The Model of Successful Meetings*, concentrating on the meaning of *potential* and its subelements of *resources* and *structure*.

3. Read the following special instructions.

Special Instructions

Team Members

In this exercise, you are a special quality improvement team in a large car dealership. You will be told by each designated facilitator what the purpose of your meeting is. During the practice session be yourselves and do not act or pretend that you are someone else. Focus on what you are trying to accomplish.

Designated Facilitators

You are the designated facilitator for a special quality improvement team. Before you begin your practice round, tell the team what they are to accomplish. You can also give the team any special instructions that you want, such as, this is its first meeting, or that the team has been working on the particular topic or problem for some time. If you want, you can build on what the previous designated facilitator has done and start your session where he/she left off. Your task as designated facilitator is to do everything that you can to help the team to strengthen its use of *resources* and its *structure*. Possible topics:

- How can we improve customer satisfaction?

- How can we cut overhead costs?

- How can we improve supplier *performance*?

- How can we strengthen the development of our own team?

- What are the blocks to our best *performance* and how can we remove them?

- How can we motivate the sales force?

- How can we improve our image with the public?

Observer/Timer

During each practice session, one team member serves as observer/timer. This person keeps the session on schedule and completes the *Observation Sheet* while observing the designated facilitator in action. If video is used, the observer/timer also operates the camera.

4. Review the *Observation Sheet* and ensure that all team members understand what they are to record on the sheet when they function as the observer/timer. The observer/timer does not participate in the practice session as a team member. He/she sits outside the team and observes the designated facilitator. At the end of the practice session the observer/timer gives feedback to the designated facilitator and gives the completed *Observation Sheet* to him/her.

5. Prepare for the practice facilitation session by assigning each member of your team (the people at your table) a letter.

Letter	Team Member
A	
B	
C	
D	
E	
F	
G	
H	

6. Review the information that follows and make sure the team knows how to proceed. During each interaction the observer/timer does the following:

- Runs the video (if used).

- Keeps time and limits the practice session to time allotted for each designated facilitator's practice session.

- Completes the *Observation Sheet* on the designated facilitator. All other members (besides the designated facilitator and the observer/timer) serve as members of the quality improvement team. Their job is to:

  - Participate in the team's discussion.

  - Observe the *performance* of the designated facilitator.

  - Participate in giving feedback to the designated facilitator at the end of the practice round.

7. Use the following schedule and conduct the exercise.

   If you use video:

   a. Conduct and tape practice interaction (<u>8</u> minutes).

   b. Discuss and give feedback (<u>4</u> minutes).

   c. Replay tape and critique (<u>8</u> minutes).

   d. Repeat steps (a) to (c) until each member has served as designated facilitator.

   If you do not use video:

   a. Conduct practice interaction (<u>8</u> minutes).

   b. Discuss and give feedback (<u>7</u> minutes).

   c. Repeat steps (a) and (b) until each member has served as designated facilitator.

Designated Facilitator	Observer/Timer* and Team Members
A	B,C,D,E,F,G*
B	C,D,E,F,G,A*
C	D,E,F,G,A,B*
D	E,F,G,A,B,C*
E	F,G,A,B,C,D*
F	G,A,B,C,D,E*
G	A,B,C,D,E,F*

   Note: Always give feedback to each designated facilitator before going on to the next practice round.

   Giving Feedback

   Remember to give useful feedback you must:

   • Be specific and concrete.

   • Be descriptive of behavior (what you see and hear).

   • Be free of opinion and interpretation.

   • Offer practical recommendations for improvement.

8. After everyone has served as a facilitator and received feedback, discuss the exercise as a team and identify three key learning points—what did you learn from doing the exercise? What would you like to remember to help you facilitate a team meeting? Bring your key learning points to the general session.

<u>**HANDOUT**</u>   **Observation Sheet (Potential)**

Fill in the name of the designated facilitator that you are observing. Make notes and respond to the questions as you observe the designated facilitator in action. Complete an *Observation Sheet* for each facilitator observed.

Facilitator Observed: _____

1. What inputs did the facilitator make that helped the team improve its use of its *resources*?

2. What inputs did the facilitator make that helped the team improve its *structure*?

3. What opportunities to help the team strengthen its *resources* or their use did the facilitator miss?

4. What opportunities to help the team strengthen its *structure* did the facilitator miss?

<u>**TRAINER'S NOTES**</u>

Practicing Facilitation, Helping Teams Perform (Communication)

Objectives

To ensure that participants understand the meaning of the element, *performance* in *The Model for Successful Meetings*, and its subelement, *communication*, and provide feedback on their skills that help a team use *quality communication*.

Description

The second element in *The Model for Successful Meetings* is *performance*. There are three subelements to this element: *quality communication, understanding,* and *rational tools*. This exercise gives participants the opportunity to recognize when a team is having problems in communicating and to make appropriate inputs to help the team improve its communication. Most problems in communication develop because team members' communication is not:

- Interactive and Balanced
- Respectful
- Concrete
- Relevant

A full discussion of these qualities is found in Chapter 2. In this exercise participants observe their colleagues during a team discussion and assess team members' inputs, by identifying those which did not meet all four criteria of quality communication. In the following exercises, participants will practice facilitating understanding and the use of rational tools.

Time

This exercise requires twenty-five minutes per team member, if video is used. It requires fifteen minutes per person if video is not used. You must also factor in time to set up the exercise. Also, participants have some individual work at the beginning of the exercise. For a six member team, the exercise will take approximately three hours. In the program designs we have limited the number of practice rounds to two. Total time for the exercise, using two rounds, is one hour.

Resources

Provide copies of the following for each participant:

- *Practicing Facilitation, Helping Teams Perform (Communication)* (p. 159)

- *Observation Sheet (Communication)* (p. 164)

Presentation

1. Review the exercise and its objectives, keeping the overhead of *The Model for Superior Facilitation* (p. 278) on the screen as you set up the exercise.

2. Assign breakout rooms, if used, and assign time to complete the exercise and return to general session.

3. Remind participants that they are learning the six competencies

identified in *The Model for Superior Facilitation*. They have learned the meaning of the first competency, *Understanding and Using the Meaning of Superior Facilitation*. They are presently working on understanding and using *The Model for Successful Meetings*. They have covered the first element in the model, *potential* and are now working on the second element, *performance*. Emphasize that in the current exercise participants will focus on the first subelement in *performance*, *communication*. This exercise gives participants the chance to use the criteria of *quality communication* by observing their team members during a discussion.

Debrief

Each team has been asked to bring at least one example of poor communication observed during the exercise. Review and discuss each of these examples.

Notes

- _____
- _____
- _____
- _____
- _____
- _____
- _____
- _____
- _____
- _____
- _____
- _____
- _____
- _____
- _____
- _____
- _____
- _____

HANDOUT

Practicing Facilitation, Helping Teams Perform (Communication)

You have _____ minutes for this exercise.

Objectives

To ensure that participants understand the meaning of the element, *performance*, in *The Model for Successful Meetings*, and its subelement, *communication*, and provide feedback on the skills that help a team use *quality communication*.

Directions

1. Review this exercise as a team and ensure that your team understands what tasks it must complete.

2. Each person works independently and spends a few moments reviewing the characteristics of *quality communication* that are found below. Note any questions that you have about the definition.

QUALITY COMMUNICATION

Teams must learn to use quality communication to achieve maximum effectiveness and efficiency in their meetings. Facilitators help them achieve such communication by their own use of quality communication. Using quality communication is a major set of competencies required for superior facilitation. The key characteristics of quality communication are:

Interactive and Balanced   Everyone is involved, no one dominates.

Concrete   What is communicated is concrete and easily understood.

Respectful   What is communicated does not target the mistakes, errors, weaknesses of members, but focuses on issues, problems, data, and goals.

Relevant   It supports what the team is doing and the team's process for doing it, i.e., content and process.

---

3. Review the *Observation Sheet* and ensure that all observer/timers understand what they are to record on the sheet. Each observer/timer will complete a sheet as he/she observes the team in action. The observer /timer will tell the team what he/she has observed at the end of each practice session.

159

4. Prepare for the practice facilitation session by assigning each member of your team (the people at your table) a letter.

Letter	Team Member
A	
B	
C	
D	
E	
F	
G	
H	

5. Review the information that follows and make sure the team knows how to proceed.

Special Instructions

Observer/Timer

During each interaction the observer/timer does the following:

- Runs the video (if used).

- Keeps time and limits the practice round to the time allowed.

- Observes the team's interaction, using the *Observation Sheet*, and notes inputs which do not meet all the criteria of quality communication.

- Shares observations with the team at the end of the practice round.

Team Members

Team members (except the observer/timer for the practice round) participate in the discussion of the assigned topic. Before each practice round, and without consulting with each other, each team member plans to make an input during the practice round that negatively illustrates one or more of the characteristics of quality communication, i.e., one that is not concrete, respectful, or relevant. During the discussion that follows each practice round, team members will share the negative quality they intended to illustrate and the statement they actually made. Write down the negative quality that you plan to illustrate in the *Planning Space* on the next page.

Planning Space (Communication)

The negative quality that I plan to illustrate is:

Practice Round #1:

Practice Round #2:

Practice Round #3:

Practice Round #4:

Practice Round #5:

Special Instructions

Designated Facilitators

For each practice round there is a designated facilitator. The designated facilitator sets the scene for each practice round. Facilitator A, sets the scene and then facilitates the practice round, followed by facilitator B, and so on until all members have functioned as designated facilitators. Designated facilitators may use one of the scenarios provided on the next page or one of their own.

4. Use the practice schedule found below and conduct the practice rounds.

If you use video:

a. Designated facilitator sets scene (3 minutes).

b. Conduct and tape practice round (10 minutes).

c. Discuss practice round, observer shares observation notes, team members share the input they made that illustrated a negative quality and give feedback (5 minutes).

d. Replay tape and critique. Replay tape selectively (7 minutes).

e. Repeat steps (a) to (d) until each member has served as designated facilitator.

If you do not use video:

a. Conduct practice interaction (10 minutes).

b. Discuss practice round, observer shares observation notes, team members share the input they made that illustrated a negative quality and give feedback (5 minutes).

c. Repeat steps 1 and 2 until each member has served as designated facilitator.

Designated Facilitator	Observer/Timer * and Team Members
A	B,C,D,E,F,G*
B	C,D,E,F,G,A*
C	D,E,F,G,A,B*
D	E,F,G,A,B,C*
E	F,G,A,B,C,D*
F	G,A,B,C,D,E*
G	A,B,C,D,E,F*

5. Select one example from your practice rounds that is a negative illustration of each of the characteristics of quality communica-

Scenarios

The team is a computer service team responsible for installing, servicing and repairing PC hardware, installing software, and assisting customers in using the software. It is meeting to generate and select ideas for improving its customer service .

The team is a total quality improvement team. It is meeting to determine how it can maintain a process of continuously improving its own development as a team .

The team is an engineering design work team responsible for designing farm machinery. It is meeting to develop ways to decrease the time that it takes from completing the design of parts to actual fabrication of the parts. Once designs are produced they are sent to the metal fabrication shop .

The team has been designated a process improvement team in a large banking chain. The team has been directed to establish its own training priorities. Earlier it developed a set of training requirements. It is meeting to prioritize these requirements. It cannot expect to go to every training program. It is realistic to expect that they can attend no more than three training programs. The training requirements the team has identified are: data collection and analysis, using control charts, creative problem solving, conducting effective meetings, work process flow charting, how to measure performance, and team leadership skills.

The team is a total quality improvement team in a large hardware chain. It is meeting to build a priority list of opportunities for improving organizational performance i.e., decrease overhead and increase market share .

The team is an intact work team responsible for developing and delivering training in the company. The team wants to ensure that the training it develops and offers is cost effective, related closely to the needs of the company and employees, and positively affects the company's performance .

HANDOUT   **Observation Sheet (Communication)**

Fill in the name of the designated facilitator that you are observing. Make notes and respond to the questions as you observe the team and the designated facilitator in action. Complete an *Observation Sheet* for each facilitator observed.

Facilitator Observed: _____

1. Record here what the facilitator did to help the team have more balanced communication.

2. Record here what the facilitator did to help the team have communication that was more concrete.

3. Record here what the facilitator did to help the team have communication that was more respectful.

4. Record here what the facilitator did to help the team have communication that was more relevant.

5. Record here any opportunities that the facilitator missed to help the team improve its communication.

<table>
<tr><td><u>TRAINER'S NOTES</u></td><td>

Practicing Facilitation, Helping Teams Perform (Developing Understanding)

</td></tr>
<tr><td>**Objectives**</td><td>

To ensure that participants are clear about the meaning of the element, *performance* in *The Model for Successful Meetings*, and its subelement, *understanding,* and provide feedback on the skills that help a team develop *understanding*.

</td></tr>
<tr><td>**Description**</td><td>

This exercise continues the process of giving participants the opportunity to demonstrate their understanding of *The Model for Successful Meetings* and how to use the model to facilitate a meeting. The second element in the model, *performance*, has three subelements. The first subelement, *quality communication*, has been covered. The second subelement, *developing understanding*, is the subject of this exercise. Participants take turns facilitating a discussion in which one or more team members does not understand what is being discussed or what the team is trying to accomplish. Designated facilitators practice understanding by helping the team become concrete, or by summarizing what the team has covered or discussed, or by making a connection the team has not made.

</td></tr>
<tr><td>**Time**</td><td>

You must allow at least twenty-five minutes for each participant to function as a facilitator, if you use videotaping and replay. Allow ten minutes per participant if you do not use video. You must also factor in time to set up the exercise. For a team of six participants, using video, this exercise will take approximately three hours.

</td></tr>
<tr><td>**Resources**</td><td>

Provide copies of the following for each participant:

- *Practicing Facilitation, Helping Teams Perform (Developing Understanding)* (p. 167)
- *The Model for Successful Meetings* (p. 278)
- *The Model for Superior Facilitation* (p. 276)
- *Developing Understanding* (p. 280)
- *Observation Sheet (Developing Understanding)* (p. 172)

</td></tr>
<tr><td>**Presentation**</td><td>

1. Review the exercise and its objectives.
2. Assign breakout rooms, if used, and assign time to complete the exercise and return to general session.
3. Use the overheads of *The Model for Superior Facilitation* (p. 276) and *The Model for Successful Meetings* (p. 278) and remind participants that they are learning to use *The Model for Successful Meetings*, which is the second competency in *The Model for Superior Facilitation*. The second element in the model is *performance*. Three subelements contribute to *performance; communication, understanding,* and the use of *rational tools*. In the previous exercise the topic was *communication*. In this exercise the topic is *understanding*.

</td></tr>
</table>

4. Use *Developing Understanding* to review the meaning of this subelement. Participants practice being facilitators, observe examples of team members not understanding, and give inputs to help team members better understand what the team is doing or discussing.

5. Review the *Observation Sheet* so that participants know what they are observing during the exercise and what information they will use as feedback.

Debrief

Each team will bring back to the general session an example that illustrates when members of a team did not understand what the team was doing or discussing and what the designated facilitator did to help the team develop understanding. Have each team give its example and have participants make comments and ask questions. The goal is to reinforce the specific characteristics of quality communication and to demonstrate the kinds of inputs that facilitators can make to help teams develop understanding.

Notes

- _____
- _____
- _____
- _____
- _____
- _____
- _____
- _____
- _____
- _____
- _____
- _____
- _____
- _____
- _____
- _____
- _____
- _____
- _____

<u>Handout</u>

Practice Facilitation, Helping Teams Perform (Developing Understanding)

You have _____ minutes for this exercise.

Objectives

To ensure that participants can identify the major inputs that can facilitate understanding and provide feedback on their demonstrated use of inputs that facilitate understanding.

Directions

1. Review this exercise as a team and ensure that your team understands what tasks it must complete.

2. Each person works independently and spends a few moments reviewing the meaning of developing understanding found below. Note any questions that you have about the definition.

Developing Understanding

The Model for Successful Meetings suggests that **performance** has three subelements which interact with each other to produce the best possible interaction during a meeting. We have described the first subelement, **quality communication**. The second subelement is **developing understanding**. Teams will move effectively and efficiently toward their goals to the degree to which members understand at all times what the team is doing and why it is doing what it is doing.

Understanding is created through the give and take of members interacting with each other. **Understanding** typically requires that information be clarified or summarized. **Understanding** is also created by making connections and showing the relationships that exist among the information and ideas produced during a meeting. A major job of facilitators is to ensure that all members at a meeting understand what is going on at all times.

Facilitators help individuals understand in a variety of ways. The most frequently used inputs in superior facilitation which stimulate and support **understanding** are inputs that clarify, summarize, and make connections.

167

INPUTS THAT CLARIFY

Inputs that clarify what is being communicated or what the team is doing stimulate and support **understanding**. One way to clarify what is being communicated is to rephrase inputs or request members to rephrase what they think another member has said. Another way is to help members become as concrete as possible in what they are communicating. Often this means something as simple as suggesting that members give examples of what they are saying .

Facilitative inputs that clarify also help keep the team co nscious of what it is doing. These are inputs that remind the team what it has set out to do, letting the team know when it has gotten side tracked, or helping the team stick to the steps or rules of a rational tool that it may be using .

INPUTS THAT SUMMARIZE

A second kind of input that helps create **understanding** is an input which summarizes information developed by the team. Facilitators may, themselves, summarize for the team what has been communicated, or what has been decided, or what action is planned. Facilitators may also encourage team members to make their own summaries .

INPUTS THAT MAKE CONNECTIONS

A third kind of input that furthers **understanding** is an input that helps team members make connections. Inputs from facilitators that help a team make connections might sound like the following: "In the light of your deciding to do A, how will that affect your earlier decision to do B?" "Do any of the causes for the problem that you have identified share anything in common?" "Do any of these strategies seem to be at odds with each other—are they all fully compatible with each other?"

3. Review the *Observation Sheet* and ensure that all observer/ timers understand what they are to record on the Sheet. Each observer/timer will complete a sheet as he/she observes the designated facilitator. The observer /timer will tell the team what he/she has observed at the end of each practice round.

4. Prepare for the practice facilitation session by assigning each member of your team (the people at your table) a letter.

Letter	Team Member
A	
B	
C	
D	
E	
F	
G	
H	

5. Review the information that follows and make sure the team knows how to proceed.

Special Instructions

Observer/Timer

During each practice round the observer/timer does the following:

- Runs the video (if used).

- Keeps time and limits the practice round to the time allowed.

- Observes the designated facilitator, using the *Observation Sheet*.

- Following each practice round, the observer/timer shares with the designated facilitator and team what he/she observed.

Designated Facilitator

Each member takes a turn being the designated facilitator. Your job as designated facilitator is to observe any situations in which team members seem not to understand what is going on, and then give an input to help the team understand what it is doing. Try to use some of the following strategies for developing understanding: clarifying, summarizing, or making connections. The designated facilitator sets the scene for each practice round. Facilitator A, sets the scene and then facilitates the practice round, followed by facilitator B, and so on until all members have functioned as designated facilitators.

Scenarios

Designated facilitators may use one of the following scenarios or one of their own.

A small publishing firm has decided that it will make a special effort to identify superior works from unpublished authors. The team's job is to:

- Identify books or topics to publish.

- Set up a process for identifying prospective superior books of unpublished authors.

The team is a computer service team required to install, service and repair PC hardware, and install software and assist customers in using the software. It is meeting to generate and select ideas for improving its services to its company customers.

The team is a total quality improvement team. It is meeting to determine how it can maintain a process of continuously improving its own development as a team.

This engineering design team is responsible for designing farm machinery. It is meeting to develop ways to decrease the time it takes from completing the design of parts to actual fabrication of the parts. Once designs are produced they are sent to the metal fabrication shop.

The team is a process improvement team in a large banking chain and has been directed to establish its training priorities. Earlier, it developed a set of training requirements. It is meeting to prioritize this set. It cannot expect to go to every training program. It is realistic to expect they can attend no more than three training programs. The set of training needs the team has identified are: data collection and analysis, using control charts, creative problem solving, conducting effective meetings, work process flowcharting, how to measure performance, and team leadership skills.

The team is an intact work team responsible for developing and delivering training in the company. The team wants to ensure that the training it develops and offers is cost effective, related closely to the needs of the company and employees, and positively affects the company's performance.

The team is a total quality improvement team in a large hardware chain. It is meeting to build a priority list of opportunities for improving the performance of the organization, i.e., decrease overhead and increase market share.

Special Instructions

Team Members

Team members (except the observer/timer and the designated facilitator for the practice round) participate in the discussion of the assigned topic. During each practice round, try to make some input which either helps create confusion or one which conveys that you don't understand what the team is doing or what it is discussing.

6. Use the practice schedule found below and conduct the practice rounds.

   If you use video:

   a. Designated facilitator sets the scene (<u>3</u> minutes).

   b. Conduct and tape practice round (<u>10</u> minutes).

   c. Discuss practice round, observer shares observation notes, team members share the input they made that illustrated confusion and give feedback (<u>5</u> minutes).

   d. Replay tape and critique. Replay tape selectively. (<u>7</u> minutes)

   e. Repeat steps (a) to (d) until each member has served as designated facilitator.

   If you do not use video:

   a. Designated facilitator sets the scene (<u>3</u> minutes).

   b. Conduct practice interaction (<u>10</u> minutes).

   c. Discuss practice round, Observer shares observation notes, team members share the input they made that illustrated confusion and give feedback (<u>7</u> minutes).

   d. Repeat steps (a) and (b) until each member has served as designated facilitator.

Designated Facilitator	Observer/Timer* and Team Members
A	B,C,D,E,F,G*
B	C,D,E,F,G,A*
C	D,E,F,G,A,B*
D	E,F,G,A,B,C*
E	F,G,A,B,C,D*
F	G,A,B,C,D,E*
G	A,B,C,D,E,F*

7. Select one example from your practice rounds that illustrates when team members did not understand what they were doing or discussing and the input made by the designated facilitator that helped team members develop understanding.

<u>**HANDOUT**</u>   **Observation Sheet (Developing Understanding)**

Fill in the name of the designated facilitator that you are observing. Make notes and respond to the questions as you observe the team and the designated facilitator in action. Complete an *Observation Sheet* for each facilitator observed.

Facilitator Observed: _____

1. Record what the facilitator did to help the team develop understanding by clarifying what it was doing or discussing.

2. Record anytime the facilitator helped the team develop understanding by making a summary of what the team was discussing or doing.

3. Record here what the facilitator did to help the team develop understanding by making a connection between actions or inputs.

4. Record any opportunities that the facilitator missed to help the team develop understanding.

TRAINER'S NOTES   # Understanding and Using Team Evaluation and Feedback

Objectives   To ensure that participants understand the third competency identified in *The Model for Superior Facilitation, Understanding and Using Team Evaluation and Feedback,* and to provide participants practice using two evaluation tools.

Description   In this exercise, participants review the meaning of team evaluation and feedback and apply two tools to their own team *performance*. They will practice evaluation during the rest of the training program by using these two tools to evaluate and improve their team's *performance*.

Time   45 minutes

Resources   Provide copies of the following for each participant:

- *Understanding and Using Team Evaluation and Feedback* (p. 174)

- *The Model for Superior Facilitation* (p. 276)

Presentation   1. Review the exercise and its objectives.

2. Assign breakout rooms, if used, and assign time to complete the exercise and return to general session.

3. Put the overhead of *The Model for Superior Facilitation* (p. 276) on the screen. Remind participants that they are learning the six competencies required for superior facilitation. Now they are working on the third competency, *Understanding and Using Evaluation and Feedback*. Review the meaning of evaluation and feedback. Information on this subject is found in Chapter 2.

Debrief   Each team will bring back to the general session their meeting norms and any questions they have about the process of evaluating team *performance* and helping teams use feedback on their *performance* to improve their meetings. Emphasize that participants will begin to use their norms and the *Team Meeting Evaluation Sheet* to evaluate and improve the way their teams meet and work together during the remainder of the workshop.

<u>**HANDOUT**</u>

**Understanding and Using
Team Evaluation and Feedback**

You have _____ minutes for this exercise.

Objectives

To ensure that participants understand the third competency identified in *The Model for Superior Facilitation*, *Understanding and Using Team Evaluation and Feedback*, and to provide participants practice using two evaluation tools.

Directions

1. Review this exercise as a team and ensure that your team understands what tasks it must complete.

2. Each team member reviews the meaning of evaluation and feedback found below.

EVALUATION AND FEEDBACK

Three conditions must always be present for teams to improve their meetings. First, members must have decided by what criteria they can judge the success of their meetings. Second they must decide how to assess their meetings, using the criteria. Third, they must assess and use the information they develop to improve their meetings.

- There are many tools that teams can use to evaluate their meetings and obtain feedback on their **performance**. Two tools for evaluating and improving team meetings that are used in this exercise are:

  — The norms that teams develop to guide its performance.
  — The elements and subelements in *The Model for Successful Meetings*.

There are many ways that teams can use these two tools to assess and improve meetings. They can use video, and occasionally tape their meetings and review their **performance**. They can use written feedback and complete a written evaluation sheet. They complete these forms anonymously, if they choose. Data is collected and summarized by the facilitator, **results** are presented to the team by the facilitator, data is discussed and opportunities and ways to improve identified. A less formal way is for the facilitator to present the criteria of evaluation and the team to reach a consensus agreement of its **performance** on each criterion.

---

3. Working as a team, select a member to facilitate this task. Use brainstorming and develop a set of norms that you think would be useful in evaluating your team meetings during the rest of this training program. Develop a final set of no more than ten norms by consensus.

4. Discuss your norms and use them to evaluate the way your team in this training program is now performing. Bring the set of norms that you developed to the general session for discussion.

5. On the following page, you will find a *Team Meeting Evaluation Sheet*. Each team member will complete the sheet and evaluate the team's meetings over the time that you have worked together during this training program. Designate a team member to serve as facilitator. Tally the team's responses. How might you improve your meetings?

6. Discuss the *Team Meeting Evaluation Sheet*. Connect the items on the sheet to *The Model for Successful Meetings*.

7. Bring your norms and any comments or questions you have about using the *Team Meeting Evaluation Sheet* to the general session for discussion.

Notes

- _____
- _____
- _____
- _____
- _____
- _____
- _____
- _____
- _____
- _____
- _____
- _____
- _____
- _____
- _____
- _____
- _____

<u>**HANDOUT**</u>   **Team Meeting Evaluation Sheet**

Circle the number which represents your response to each item:	**Agree**				**Disagree**
1. We used everyone as a resource.	5	4	3	2	1
2. We used our time effectively.	5	4	3	2	1
3. We made good use of the information available to us.	5	4	3	2	1
4. We adhered to our team meeting norms.	5	4	3	2	1
5. We stayed focused on our tasks.	5	4	3	2	1
6. We followed logical steps in conducting our discussions.	5	4	3	2	1
7. We listened to each other.	5	4	3	2	1
8. We resolved our differences in opinion positively.	5	4	3	2	1
9. Our conversation was typically concrete.	5	4	3	2	1
10. No person dominated the conversation.	5	4	3	2	1

Comments:

_____

_____

_____

_____

_____

_____

_____

_____

_____

_____

_____

_____

_____

_____

_____

Practicing Quality Communication

Objectives

To ensure that participants understand the fourth competency identified in *The Model for Superior Facilitation, Modeling and Using Quality Communication*, and to provide feedback on their skill in using quality communication.

Description

In previous exercises, participants have covered the first three competencies, identified in *The Model for Superior Facilitation*. In this exercise, participants review the meaning of quality communication and then receive feedback on how well they use quality communication. Participants conduct a discussion as a team. One member serves as the designated facilitator. During the discussion, team members are observed by an observer/timer.

Time

45 minutes

Resources

Provide copies of the following for each participant:

- *Practicing Quality Communication* (p. 178)

- *Observation Sheet (Quality Communication)* (p. 181)

- *The Model for Superior Facilitation* (p. 276)

- *Quality Communication* (p. 279)

Presentation

1. Review the exercise and its objectives.

2. Assign breakout rooms, if used, and assign time to complete the exercise and return to general session.

3. Put the overhead of *The Model for Superior Facilitation* (p. 276) on the screen. Remind participants that they are learning the six competencies required for superior facilitation. They are working on the fourth competency, *Modeling and Using Quality Communication*.

4. Use the overhead, *Quality Communication* (p. 279) to review the characteristics of quality communication.

5. Go over the *Observation Sheet* that the observer/timer will use for this exercise so that everyone is clear about what is being observed.

Debrief

Each team will bring back to the general session an example that illustrates when members of a team did not use quality communication during the practice session. Review each example and the reasons that the example was poor communication, i.e., was not balanced, or concrete, or respectful, or relevant.

<u>HANDOUT</u>

Practicing Quality Communication

You have _____ minutes for this exercise.

Objectives

To ensure that participants understand the fourth competency identified in *The Model for Superior Facilitation, Modeling and Using Quality Communication,* and to provide feedback on their skill in using quality communication.

Directions

1. Review this exercise as a team to ensure that your team understands what tasks it must complete.

2. Each person works independently and spends a few moments reviewing the characteristics of quality communication that are found below. Note any questions that you have about the definition.

QUALITY COMMUNICATION

Teams must learn to use quality communication to achieve maximum effectiveness and efficiency in their meetings. Facilitators help them achieve such communication by their own use of quality communication. Using quality communication is a major set of competencies required for superior facilitation. The key characteristics of quality communication are:

Interactive and Balanced   Everyone is involved, no one dominates.

Concrete   What is communicated is concrete and easily understood.

Respectful   What is communicated does not target the mistakes, errors, weaknesses of members, but focuses on issues, problems, data, and goals.

Relevant   It supports what the team is doing and the process for doing it, i.e., content and process.

---

3. Review the *Observation Sheet* to ensure that team members understand what behaviors are being observed during the exercise. The observer/timer will complete the *Observation Sheet* while observing the team in a practice discussion. At the end of the practice discussion, the observer/timer will give feedback to team members regarding what he/she has observed.

4. Prepare for the practice discussion by designating the observer/timer.

5. Review the information that follows and make sure the team knows how to proceed.

Special Instructions

Observer/Timer

One team member will be the observer/timer during the practice round. The observer/timer does the following:

- Keeps time and limits the practice round to the time allowed.

- Observes the team's interaction, using the *Observation Sheet*, and notes inputs which do not meet all the criteria of quality communication.

- Shares observations with the team at the end of the practice round.

Team Members

Team members (except the observer/timer) participate in a practice discussion. Assume that you are a team in a textile mill (made up of managers and employees) that has been given the task of helping the company move away from a "command and control" style of management to one which will make fuller use of the ideas and experience of employees. The immediate reason for putting the team together is that management decided to computerize the personnel information system, without using employee input, which ended with disastrous *results*. Before the practice session discussion begins, and without consulting with each other, each team member plans to make an input during the practice round that negatively illustrates one or more of the characteristics of quality communication, i.e., one that is not concrete, respectful, or relevant. During the discussion that follows each practice round, team members will share the negative quality they intended to illustrate and the statement they actually made. Write down the negative quality that you plan to illustrate in the *Planning Space* on the next page.

<u>**HANDOUT**</u>   **Planning Space (Quality Communication)**

The negative quality that I plan to illustrate during the practice discussion is:

Schedule

1. Conduct practice interaction (<u>20</u> minutes).

2. Discuss practice round, observer shares observation notes, team members share the input they made that illustrated a negative quality and give feedback (<u>15</u> minutes).

3. Observer/timer prepares the *Observation Sheet*.

4. Conduct the practice discussion. Observer/timer makes observations and records them.

5. Observer/timer shares observations and gives feedback to team members.

6. Team members share the input that they intended to make and the input that they did make that was a negative illustration of quality communication.

7. Select one example from your practice round that is a negative illustration of each of the characteristics of quality communication. Bring your examples to the general session.

Observation Sheet (Quality Communication)

The observer/timer uses this sheet to record any examples observed which are negative illustrations of the characteristics of quality communication. In the left-hand column, write the initials of the team member making the input. Record in the second column a few notes to help you remember the input made. In the right-hand column, circle the negative qualities that the input illustrates.

Team Member	Input	The Input Was Not
		Balanced Respectful Concrete Relevant
		Balanced Respectful Concrete Relevant
		Balanced Respectful Concrete Relevant
		Balanced Respectful Concrete Relevant
		Balanced Respectful Concrete Relevant
		Balanced Respectful Concrete Relevant
		Balanced Respectful Concrete Relevant
		Balanced Respectful Concrete Relevant
		Balanced Respectful Concrete Relevant
		Balanced Respectful Concrete Relevant
		Balanced Respectful Concrete Relevant
		Balanced Respectful Concrete Relevant
		Balanced Respectful Concrete Relevant
		Balanced Respectful Concrete Relevant
		Balanced Respectful Concrete Relevant
		Balanced Respectful Concrete Relevant
		Balanced Respectful Concrete Relevant
		Balanced Respectful Concrete Relevant

Understanding and Practicing the Special Functions of Facilitation

Objectives

To ensure that participants understand the fifth competency identified in *The Model for Superior Facilitation, Understanding and Using the Special Functions of Facilitator,* and provide feedback on their skill in using the special function of *mediator.*

Description

In previous exercises, participants have covered the first four competencies, identified in *The Model for Superior Facilitation*. In this exercise, participants review the meaning of the special functions of facilitation and then practice these functions. One team member serves as designated facilitator. Any of the functions can be practiced, but we have selected the function of mediator. A full discussion of the special functions is found in Chapter 2. Teams will use their norms and the *Team Meeting Evaluation Sheet* (p. 191) to evaluate their meeting and look for ways to improve the way they are working together.

Time

1 hour

Resources

Provide copies of the following for each participant:

- *Understanding and Practicing the Special Functions of Facilitation* (p. 183)

- *Observation Sheet (Special Functions)* (p. 190)

- *Team Meeting Evaluation Sheet* (p. 191)

- *The Model for Superior Facilitation* (p. 276)

- *Special Facilitation Functions* (p. 281)

Presentation

1. Review the exercise and its objectives.

2. Assign breakout rooms, if used, and assign time to complete the exercise and return to general session.

3. Using the overhead, *The Model for Superior Facilitation* (p. 276), remind participants that they are learning the six competencies required for superior facilitation. Then, using the overhead, *Special Facilitation Functions* (p. 281), review the meaning of each of the functions.

4. Go over the *Observation Sheet* that the observer/timer will use for this exercise so that everyone is clear about what is being observed.

Debrief

Each team will bring back to the general session three key learnings from the exercise. Review and discuss each of the learnings.

(Information on the technique *Brainstorming* is found page 242.)

HANDOUT

Understanding and Practicing the Special Functions of Facilitation

You have _____ minutes for this exercise.

Objectives

To ensure that participants understand the fifth competency identified in *The Model for Superior Facilitation*, *Understanding and Using the Special Functions of Facilitation*, and provide feedback on their skill in using one of the special functions, *mediator*.

Directions

1. Review this exercise as a team to ensure that your team understands what tasks it must complete.

2. Each team member takes five minutes to review the following definition of the *Special Functions of Facilitation*.

3. Discuss as a team each of the special functions to ensure that there is a common understanding among team members of the meaning of each function. Review a second time the meaning of *mediator*. This time, ensure that members have a good idea of the steps to follow in mediating conflict. In this exercise one team member will serve as designated facilitator and practice mediating a conflict. If there is time, of course, the exercise can be repeated so that other members can practice this function.

4. Review the *Observation Sheet* and ensure that team members understand what behaviors are being observed during the exercise. The observer/timer will complete the *Observation Sheet* while observing the designated facilitator in action. At the end of the practice discussion, the observer/timer gives feedback to designated facilitator and team members discuss and learn from observations.

5. Prepare for the practice discussion by designating the observer/timer. Get a volunteer to serve as designated facilitator.

6. Review the information that follows and make sure the team knows how to proceed.

SPECIAL FUNCTIONS OF FACILITATION

In addition to their primary function, facilitators may, on occasion, perform certain special functions. These are:

- Be a resource providing special information to the team .
- Be a teacher when teams need to learn a new skill, like using a rational tool.
- Be a mediator when individuals get at cross purposes or become conflicted over an issue.
- Be a challenger who suggests the team goes beyond what they have achieved to attempt a more difficult task or goal .

Special Function #1

BE A RESOURCE

A facilitator need not be an expert in the particular subject that occupies a team. But a facilitator may well be such an expert. Either way, there may be times in which a question of fact may arise. Questions like, "Who has that responsibility in the company?" "Is there data available about this problem?" "Which companies are the best benchmarks for this process?" "What tools can we use to develop the information we need?" When facilitators are asked such questions, they should put the question back to the team to find out if some members might be a resource. When members do not know answers to questions of fact and the facilitator does, then the facilitator takes on the special function of resource .

Special Function #2

BE A TEACHER

The need to function as a teacher arises most often in rel a-tion to helping the team members learn a new skill related to improving their ability to conduct meetings. When facilitators expect to work with teams over a period, one of the most useful things that facilitators can do is to introduce members to *The Model for Successful Meetings*. When members all work with a common **understanding** of the kind of meeting they are trying to create, they have begun the very powerful process of developing each member as a facilitator and hel p-ing the team assume responsibility for its own facilitation .

In addition to teaching members how to us e *The Model for Successful Meetings*, facilitators can teach members how to use various rational tools to develop information and solve problems. We will discuss the specific tools that facilitators should know how to use when we come to examine the sixth competency, **understanding** and using rational tools .

Special Function #3

BE A MEDIATOR

Strong disagreement and even conflict can develop among members of a team during a meeting. If the behaviors of members create blocks to the progress of a meeting toward its goals, facilitators can become mediators and help members resolve their differences.

Special Function #4

BE A CHALLENGER

Teams never know what they can achieve until the members learn to work easily and well together. If you think of *The Model for Successful Meetings*, teams can always increase their potential for achieving superior **results** and can learn to perform or interact at higher and higher levels of efficiency and effectiveness. There can occur times, therefore, when it is useful for facilitators to help teams recognize their capacity to do more than they have done and to take on more and more challenging tasks and goals.

There are an unlimited number of ways that a team can improve its meetings. Teams can learn to use more and more kinds of rational tools. A process improvement team may, for example, start out by charting the steps in a process and then looking for opportunities to reduce the number of operations in the process, or eliminate waste and delay. Later, a facilitator might challenge the team to learn how to use statistical control charts to monitor and improve the process.

Mediating Conflict

If teams have included how disagreements and conflicts will be resolved in their norms as part of the process of structuring their meetings, the facilitator may have to do little more than remind members of their norms. If it is not possible to refer to norms, or if such reference doesn't work, the facilitator can proceed as follows:

1. Give the team the opportunity to decide whether it can proceed without resolving the conflict and come back to it later. Often conflicts at one point in a process become irrelevant as a meeting progresses. Also, members are often able to resolve their differences at a later time. The conditions that created the conflict may have changed and the conflict or disagreement may have *dissolved*.

2. If the team feels the conflict must be resolved before the meeting can proceed, the facilitator can propose a process of win-win resolution. Your goals as a mediator are:

    • Involve the whole team in the process of resolution, i.e., depersonalize the problem.

    • Find a win-win solution to the disagreement or conflict.

    • Here is how to proceed, once the team has committed to finding a solution to the disagreement.

3. Explain to the team how you intend to proceed. Put the steps shown below on chart paper. Ensure understanding and agreement.

4. Divide the team into two subgroups.

5. Have each subgroup take some time to formulate as clearly and as concretely as possible a statement of the problem. Have each subgroup write an answer to the following: "What are the two positions? What does "A" want or think? What does "B" want or think? The goal here is to make sure that there is a problem, i.e., real disagreement.

6. Have each subgroup put its statement of the two positions on chart paper. Facilitate a discussion of the statements. Give subgroups the opportunity to modify what they have written. You may find that there is no real disagreement, only a misunderstanding of the problem.

7. Next use brainstorming and develop a list of agreements between the two positions.

8. Now use brainstorming and develop a list of disagreements between the two positions. You may find now that the disagreements are trivial and that it is easy to reach a consensus.

9. If no agreement has been reached by this step, ask each subgroup to generate solutions that could satisfy people representing both positions. Have each subgroup place its solutions on chart paper.

10. Look for agreement or close agreement in the solutions. Select (as with every other step, by consensus) the most acceptable solution. You may find that solutions are combined and modified in this step.

Discuss the solution until it is stated in a form that "everyone can live with."

Special Instructions

Observer/Timer

One team member will be the observer/timer. During each interaction the observer/timer does the following:

• Runs the video (if you use it).

• Keeps time and limits the practice round to the time allowed.

• Observe the designated facilitator using the *Observation Sheet* and makes notes.

• Shares observations with the designated facilitator and team at the end of the practice round.

Team Members

Team members (except the designated Facilitator and observer/timer) participate in a practice discussion. Assume that your team has been established to determine whether or not there should be a trained pool of facilitators in your company to facilitate the many total quality and continuous improvement teams that are being organized. Have half of the team represent position 'X'. They feel strongly that there must be a pool of trained facilitators who can be called on by any team to obtain a facilitator. Have half of the team represent position 'Y'. They feel that each team should develop its own facilitator or that the team should learn to manage without a facilitator. During the practice interaction, members should support their position, but should not be artificial. Be yourselves.

Designated Facilitator

Your job is to mediate the conflict and come up with a solution that satisfies both groups 'X' and 'Y'. You follow the process for resolving conflicts outlined above under the special function of mediator. You are helping the whole team learn how to use the process for resolving conflict. The other members will learn from what you do.

If you use video:

a. Conduct and tape practice interaction (<u>25</u> minutes). The observer/timer will observe and take notes using the *Observation Sheet*.

b. Observer/timer gives feedback (<u>10</u> minutes).

c. Selectively replay portions of tape and critique (<u>10</u> minutes).

If you do not use video:

a. Conduct and tape practice interaction (<u>30</u> minutes). Observer/timer observes and takes notes using the *Observation Sheet*.

b. Observer/timer gives feedback (<u>15</u> minutes).

11. Before you begin the practice session, assign half of the team to position 'X' (for a pool of facilitators) and half of the them to position 'Y' (against a pool of facilitators). Team members take a few minutes before the practice session begins and jot down as many reasons as they can to support their assigned position.

My Assigned Position is:

_____

Reasons that support this position are:

_____

_____

_____

_____

_____

_____

_____

_____

12. Conduct the practice session. Have the team start discussing the problem for five minutes. They take their assigned positions and develop clear disagreement. Then the facilitator indicates that there appears to be a serious disagreement and follows the steps below.

a. Explain to the team how you intend to proceed. Put the steps shown below on chart paper. Ensure understanding and agreement.

    b. Divide the team into two subgroups.

    c. Have each subgroup take some time to formulate as clearly and as concretely as possible a statement of the problem. Have each subgroup write an answer to the following: "What are the two positions? What does 'X' want or think? What does 'Y' want or think? The goal here is to make sure that there is a problem, i.e., real disagreement.

    d. Have each subgroup put its statement of the two positions on chart paper. Facilitate a discussion of the statements. Give subgroups the opportunity to modify what they have written. You may find that there is no real disagreement, only a misunderstanding of the problem.

    e. Next use brainstorming and develop a list of agreements between the two positions.

    f. Now use brainstorming and develop a list of disagreements between the two positions. You may find now that the disagreements are trivial and that it is easy to reach a consensus.

    g. If no agreement has been reached by this step, ask each subgroup to generate solutions that could satisfy people representing both positions. Have each subgroup place its solutions on chart paper.

    h. Look for agreement or close agreement in the solutions. Select (as with every other step, by consensus) the most acceptable solution. You may find that solutions are combined and modified in this step.

    i. Discuss the solution until it is stated in a form that "everyone can live with."

13. Observer/Timer calls "time" to end practice discussion and then shares with the designated facilitator and the team his/her observations.

14. Team identifies three key learning points from the exercise to bring to the general session for discussion. Designate a facilitator to use team norms and the *Team Meeting Evaluation Sheet* to evaluate the way your team is meeting and how you might improve.

15. Team uses the *Team Meeting Evaluation Sheet* and evaluates the meeting.

HANDOUT   **Observation Sheet (Special Functions)**

The observer/timer completes this while observing the designated facilitator mediate the conflict in the team.

1. What was the quality of the designated facilitator's communication with the team? Was it concrete? Respectful? Relevant? Give positive and negative examples.

2. How well did the designated facilitator describe how she/he was going to proceed to help the team resolve its conflict? How might this have been improved?

3. Did the designated facilitator keep the team on track and follow the steps outlined for mediating conflict? Give positive and negative examples.

4. Did the designated facilitator help the team resolve its conflict or move the team toward resolving its conflict?

5. Did the designated facilitator help the team move toward a win/win solution? What was the solution?

6. What comments do you have that might help all of your team members manage the process of resolving conflict?

<u>**HANDOUT**</u>   **Team Meeting Evaluation Sheet**

Circle the number which represents your response to each item:	Agree				Disagree
1. We used everyone as a resource.	5	4	3	2	1
2. We used our time effectively.	5	4	3	2	1
3. We made good use of the information available to us.	5	4	3	2	1
4. We adhered to our team meeting norms.	5	4	3	2	1
5. We stayed focused on our tasks.	5	4	3	2	1
6. We followed logical steps in conducting our discussions.	5	4	3	2	1
7. We listened to each other.	5	4	3	2	1
8. We resolved our differences in opinion positively.	5	4	3	2	1
9. Our conversation was typically concrete.	5	4	3	2	1
10. No person dominated the conversation.	5	4	3	2	1

Comments:

_____

_____

_____

_____

_____

_____

_____

_____

_____

_____

_____

_____

_____

_____

_____

_____

<u>TRAINER'S NOTES</u>

Understanding and Practicing Rational Tools (Developing Information and Ideas)

Objectives

To ensure that participants understand the sixth competency identified in *The Model for Superior Facilitation*, *Understanding and Using Rational Tools,* and to provide feedback on their skill in using rational tools to develop information and ideas.

Description

In previous exercises, participants have covered the first five competencies identified in *The Model for Superior Facilitation*. This is a generic exercise in using rational tools. The same exercise can be used for each of the rational tools described in Chapter 10. In this exercise, participants review the meaning of rational tools and then practice using them for developing information and ideas. In the next exercises they will practice using tools for making decisions and evaluating alternatives, and improving quality. Participants serve as designated facilitators, practice helping their team use a rational tool, and then receive feedback on their *performance*.

The tools for generating information and ideas are:

- *Brainstorming* (p. 242).

- *Nominal Group Technique* (p. 243).

- *Gallery Method* (p. 245).

The tools for making decisions and evaluating alternatives are:

- *Consensus Decision Making* (p. 247).

- *Plus-and-Minus Technique* (p. 248).

- *Priority Analysis* (p. 250).

The following tools for quality improvement are:

- *Flowcharting* (p. 254).

- *Cause-and-Effect Diagrams* (p. 258).

- *Pareto Charts* (p. 260).

Time

This exercise may be repeated three times to provide practice using all three tools. The practice round takes forty-five minutes. You must allow additional time for setting up the exercise. You should allow two hours and forty-five minutes, if you use all three practice rounds. In the program designs in this sourcebook, we have allocated one hour for a single practice round.

Resources

Provide copies of the following for each participant:

- *Understanding and Practicing Rational Tools (Developing Information and Ideas) (p. 194)*

- *Types of Rational Tools* (p. 282)

- *Tools for Generating Information and Ideas* (p. 283)

- *Tools for Generating Information and Ideas* (p. 241)

- *Observation Sheet (Developing Information and Ideas)* (p. 197) three copies per participant.

Additional Supplies

- Flipchart and paper for practicing Brainstorming.

- 3x5 cards for practicing the Nominal Group Technique.

- Flipchart paper, markers, and tape for practicing the Gallery Method.

Presentation

1. Review the exercise and its objectives.

2. Assign breakout rooms, if used, and assign time to complete the exercise and return to general session.

3. Put the overhead of *The Model for Superior Facilitation* (p. 276) on the screen and remind participants that they are learning the six competencies required for superior facilitation. They have covered the first five competencies. Now they are working on the sixth and last competency, *Understanding and Using Rational Tools*.

4. Use the overhead, *Types of Rational Tools* (p. 282) to review the three kinds of tools. Emphasize that they will be working on the first kind of tool, ones for developing information and ideas.

5. Use the overhead, *Tools for Generating Information and Ideas* (p. 283) to review these tools.

6. Go over the *Observation Sheet* that team members will use for this exercise so that everyone is clear about what is being observed.

Debrief

Each team will bring back to the general session questions about the tools that they have practiced using. They also bring back information about how they might use the tool. Review and respond to questions and review possible uses of the tool.

Understanding and Practicing Rational Tools (Developing Information and Ideas)

You have _____ minutes for this exercise.

Objectives

To ensure that participants understand the sixth competency identified in *The Model for Superior Facilitation, Understanding and Using Rational Tools,* and to provide feedback on their skill in using rational tools to develop information and ideas.

Directions

1. Review this exercise as a team and ensure that your team understands what tasks it must complete.

2. Each team member takes fifteen minutes to review the descriptions of the following rational tools for developing information and ideas:

    •   Brainstorming

    •   Nominal Group Technique

    •   Gallery Method

3. Review and discuss each of the tools as a team and ensure that each team member understands these tools.

4. Prepare for the facilitation practice rounds by having three team members volunteer to use one of the three rational tools for developing information and ideas. Facilitator "A" facilitates the first practice round, facilitator "B" the next, and facilitator "C" the final practice round.

Team Member	Letter	Tool
	A	Brainstorming
	B	Nominal Group Technique
	C	Gallery Method

5. Review as a team the *Observation Sheet*. Each team member will complete this sheet at the end of each practice round. There are three practice rounds and there are three copies of the *Observation Sheet*.

6. The designated facilitator sets the scene for practicing the rational tool. The facilitator may set his/her own scene or use the scenarios on the next page.

7. Review the special instructions that follow and make sure the team knows how to proceed.

Scenarios

SUITABLE FOR BRAINSTORMING

The team is a computer service team required to install, service and repair PC hardware, and install software and assist customers in using the software. It is meeting to generate and select ideas for improving its services to its company customers.

SUITABLE FOR NOMINAL GROUP TECHNIQUE

The team is a total quality improvement team. It is meeting to determine how it can maintain a process of continuously improving its own development as a team.

SUITABLE FOR GALLERY METHOD

The team is an engineering design work responsible to design farm machinery. It is meeting to develop ways to decrease the time that it takes from completing the design of parts to actual fabrication of the parts. Once designs are produced they are sent to the metal fabrication shop.

Special Instructions

Timer

Appoint a timer for each practice round. During each interaction the timer keeps time, limiting each practice round to thirty minutes, followed by ten minutes of feedback and discussion.

Team Members

Team members use the rational tool being practiced and try to learn for themselves as much as possible about its use. At the end of each practice round each team member completes a copy of the *Observation Sheet*. These observation sheets become the basis for the team's discussion following each practice round. All those who are not designated a facilitator are members of the teams being facilitated.

Designated Facilitator

The designated facilitator practices using the assigned rational tool and facilitates the team's use of the tool. There will be three practice rounds in this exercise and three designated facilitators. Each will practice the use of one of the following rational tools:

- Brainstorming

- Nominal Group Technique

- Gallery Method

8. Follow the schedule below and complete the exercise.

   a. The designated facilitator sets the scene for the practice round (5 minutes).

   b. Conduct practice interaction (30 minutes).

   c. Discuss and give feedback (10 minutes).

   d. Repeat steps (a) to (c) for all three practice rounds.

9. Work as a team to identify any questions that you have about using any of the rational tools used in the exercise. Summarize your thoughts about when you might use the tool (Question 6 in the *Observation Sheet*).

<u>HANDOUT</u>   **Observation Sheet (Developing Information/Ideas)**

This sheet is to be completed by all team members, including the designated facilitator, at the end of each practice round. After completing the *Observation Sheet*, the team will discuss its experience of learning to use the rational tool.

1. How clearly did the designated facilitator present the purpose of the practice round, i.e., the setting and what the team was meeting to accomplish? If this step could have been improved, how might it have been improved?

2. How clearly did the designated facilitator set up the steps for using the rational tool? If this step could have been improved, how might it have been improved?

3. Did the team become confused at any time in using the rational tool? What was the confusion? How did it occur? How might it have been avoided?

4. Did the designated facilitator keep the team on track, i.e., following the steps of the rational tool in the correct sequence? If this step could have been improved, how might it have been improved?

5. What question do you have about the best way to use this tool?

6. Where, in your own experience with team meetings, might this tool be used?

Understanding and Practicing Rational Tools (Making Decisions and Evaluating Alternatives)

Objectives

To ensure that participants understand the sixth competency identified in *The Model for Superior Facilitation, Understanding and Using Rational Tools,* and to provide feedback on their skill in using rational tools to make decisions and evaluate alternatives.

Description

In previous exercises, participants have covered the first five competencies identified in *The Model for Superior Facilitation.* This is a generic exercise in rational tools. The same exercise can be used for each of the rational tools described in Chapter 10. In this exercise, participants review the meaning of rational tools and then one participant practices using one tool for making decisions and evaluating alternatives. In the next exercises they will practice using tools for quality improvement. The rational tools covered in this book are found in Chapter 10. Participants serve as designated facilitators, practice helping their team use a rational tool, and receive feedback on their *performance.* The tools for generating information and ideas are:

- *Brainstorming* (p. 242).

- *Nominal Group Technique* (p. 243).

- *Gallery Method* (p. 245).

The tools for making decisions and evaluating alternatives are:

- *Consensus Decision Making* (p. 247).

- *Plus-and-Minus Technique* (p. 248).

- *Priority Analysis* (p. 250).

The tools for quality improvement are:

- *Flowcharting* (p. 254).

- *Cause-and-Effect Diagrams* (p. 258).

- *Pareto Charts* (p. 260).

Time

This exercise may be repeated three times to provide practice in all three tools. The practice round takes forty-five minutes. You must allow additional time for setting up the exercise. You should allow two hours and forty-five minutes, if you use all three practice rounds. In the program designs in this sourcebook, we have allowed for a single practice round and allocated one hour.

Resources	Provide copies of the following for each participant:

- *Understanding and Practicing Rational Tools (Making Decisions and Evaluating Alternatives)* (p. 200)

- *Tools for Making Decisions and Evaluating Alternatives* (p. 246)

- *Observation Sheet (Making Decisions/Alternatives)* (p. 203)

- *Priority Analysis Sheet (Blank)*, if used (p. 252)

- *Types of Rational Tools* (p. 282)

- *Tools for Making Decisions and Evaluating Alternatives* (p. 284)

- Blank paper for Plus-and-Minus Technique if used.

Presentation

1. Review the exercise and its objectives.

2. Assign breakout rooms, if used, and assign time to complete the exercise and return to general session.

3. Put the overhead of *The Model for Superior Facilitation* (p. 276) on the screen. Remind participants that they are learning the six competencies required for superior facilitation. They have covered the first five competencies. Now they are working on the sixth competency, *Understanding and Using Rational Tools*.

4. Use the overhead, *Types of Rational Tools* (p. 282) to review the three kinds of tools. Emphasize that they will be working on the second kind of tool, used for making decisions and evaluating alternatives.

5. Review these tools using the overhead, *Tools for Making Decisions and Evaluating Alternatives* (p. 284).

6. Go over the *Observation Sheet* that team members will use for this exercise so that everyone is clear about what is being observed.

Debrief

Each team will bring back to the general session questions about the tools that they have practiced using. They also bring back information about how they might use the tool. Review and respond to questions, and review possible uses of the tool.

<u>HANDOUT</u>

Understanding and Practicing Rational Tools (Making Decisions and Evaluating Alternatives)

You have _____ minutes for this exercise.

Objectives

To ensure that participants understand the sixth competency identified in *The Model for Superior Facilitation, Understanding and Using Rational Tools,* and to provide feedback on their skill in using rational tools to make decisions and evaluate alternatives.

Directions

1. Review this exercise as a team to ensure that your team understands what tasks it must complete.

2. Each team member will take fifteen minutes to review the descriptions of the following rational tools for making decisions and evaluating alternatives:

   • Consensus Decision Making

   • Plus-and-Minus Technique

   • Priority Analysis

3. Review and discuss each of the tools as a team and ensure that each team member understands these tools.

4. Prepare for the facilitation practice rounds by having three team members volunteer to use one of the three rational tools for making decisions and evaluating alternatives. Facilitator 'A' facilitates the first practice round, facilitator 'B' the next, and facilitator 'C' the final practice round.

Team Member	Letter	Tool
	A	Consensus Decision Making
	B	Plus-and-Minus Technique
	C	Priority Analysis

5. Review as a team the *Observation Sheet*. Each team member will complete this sheet at the end of each practice round. There are three practice rounds, and there are three copies of the *Observation Sheet*.

6. The designated facilitator sets the scene for practicing the rational tool. The facilitator may set his/her own scene or use one of the scenarios provided.

7. Review the special instructions that follow and make sure the team knows how to proceed.

Special Instructions

Timer

Appoint a timer for each practice round. During each interaction the timer keeps time, limits each practice round to thirty minutes, followed by ten minutes of feedback and discussion.

Team Members

Team members use the rational tool being practiced and try to learn for themselves as much as they can about using the tool. At the end of each practice round each team member completes a copy of the *Observation Sheet*. These observation sheets become the basis for the team's discussion following each practice round. All those who are not the designated facilitator are members of the team being facilitated.

Facilitator

The facilitator practices using the assigned rational tool and facilitates the team's use of the tool. There will be three practice rounds in this exercise and three designated facilitators who will each practice the use of one of the following rational tools:

- Consensus Decision Making

- Plus-and-Minus Technique

- Priority Analysis

8. Follow the schedule below and complete the exercise.

   a. The designated facilitator sets the scene for the practice round (5 minutes).

   b. Conduct practice interaction (30 minutes).

   c. Discuss and give feedback (10 minutes).

   d. Repeat steps (a) to (c) for all three practice rounds.

9. Working as a team, identify any questions that you have about using any of the rational tools used in the exercise. Summarize your thoughts about when you might use the tool (Question 6 in the *Observation Sheet*).

Scenarios

SUITABLE FOR CONSENSUS DECISION MAKING

The team has been designated a process improvement team in a large banking chain. The team has been directed to establish its own training priorities. Earlier it developed a set of training requirements. It is meeting to prioritize this set. It cannot expect to go to every training program. It is realistic to expect that they can attend no more than three training programs. The set of training needs that the team has identified are:

- Data collection and analysis
- Using control charts
- Creative problem solving
- Conducting effective meetings
- Work process flow charting
- How to measure performance
- Team leadership skills

SUITABLE FOR PLUS-AND-MINUS TECHNIQUE

The team is an intact work team responsible for developing and delivering training in the company. The team wants to ensure that the training it develops and offers is cost effective, related closely to the needs of the company and employees, and positively affects the company's performance.

SUITABLE FOR PRIORITY ANALYSIS

The team is a total quality improvement team in a large hardware chain. It is meeting to build a priority list of opportunities for improving the performance of the organization, i.e., decrease overhead and increase market share.

HANDOUT   **Observation Sheet (Making Decisions/Alternatives)**

This sheet is to be completed by all team members, including the designated facilitator, at the end of each practice round. After each team member has taken a few moments to complete the *Observation Sheet*, the team discusses its experience learning to use the rational tool.

1. How clearly did the designated facilitator present the purpose of the practice round, i.e., the setting and what the team was meeting to accomplish? If this step could have been improved, how might it have been improved?

2. How clearly did the designated facilitator set up the steps for using the rational tool? If this step could have been improved, how might it have been improved?

3. Did the team become confused at any time in using the rational tool? What was the confusion? How did it occur? How might it have been avoided?

4. Did the designated facilitator keep the team on track, i.e., following the steps in the rational tool in the correct sequence? If this step could have been improved, how might it have been improved?

5. What question do you have about the best way to use this tool?

6. Where, in your own experience with team meetings, might this tool be used?

Understanding and Practicing Rational Tools (Quality Improvement)

Objectives

To ensure that participants understand the sixth competency identified in *The Model for Superior Facilitation*, *Understanding and Using Rational Tools*, and provide feedback on their skill in using rational tools for quality improvement.

Description

In previous exercises, participants have covered the first four competencies identified in *The Model for Superior Facilitation*. This is a generic exercise in rational tools. The same exercise can be used for each of the rational tools described in Chapter 10. In this exercise, participants review the meaning of tools for quality improvement. Participants serve as designated facilitators, practice helping their team use a rational tool, and receive feedback on their *performance*. The tools for generating information and ideas are:

- *Brainstorming* (p. 242)

- *Nominal Group Technique* (p. 243)

- *Gallery Method* (p. 245)

The tools for making decisions and evaluating alternatives are:

- *Consensus Decision Making* (p. 247)

- *Plus-and-Minus Technique* (p. 248)

- *Priority Analysis* (p. 250)

The tools for quality improvement are:

- *Flowcharting* (p. 254)

- *Cause-and-Effect Diagrams* (p. 258)

- *Pareto Charts* (p. 260)

Time

This exercise may be repeated three times to provide practice in all three tools. The practice round takes forty-five minutes. You must allow additional time for setting up the exercise. You should allow two hours and forty-five minutes, if you use all three practice rounds. In the program designs in this sourcebook, we have allowed for a single practice round and allocated one hour.

Resources   Provide copies of the following for each participant:

- *Understanding and Practicing Rational Tools (Quality Improvement)* (p. 206)

- *Types of Rational Tools* (p. 282)

- *Tools for Quality Improvement* (p. 285)

- *Tools for Quality Improvement* (p. 253)

- *Observation Sheet (Quality Improvement)* (p. 209) three per participant.

- Graph paper for making Pareto charts.

Presentation   1. Review the exercise and its objectives.

2. Assign breakout rooms, if used, and assign time to complete the exercise and return to general session.

3. Put the overhead of *The Model for Superior Facilitation* (p. 276) on the screen. Remind participants that they are learning the six competencies required for superior facilitation. They have covered the first five competencies. Now they are working on the sixth competency, *Understanding and Using Rational Tools.*

4. Use the overhead, *Types of Rational Tools* (p. 282) to review the three kinds of tools.

5. Use the overhead, *Tools for Quality Improvement* (p. 285) to review these tools.

6. Go over the *Observation Sheet* that team members will use for this exercise so that everyone is clear about what is being observed.

Debrief   Each team will bring back to the general session questions about the tools that they have practiced using. They also bring back information about how they might use the tool. Review and respond to questions, and review possible uses of the tool.

<u>HANDOUT</u>

Understanding and Practicing Rational Tools (Quality Improvement)

You have _____ minutes for this exercise.

Objectives

To ensure that participants understand the sixth competency identified in *The Model for Superior Facilitation, Understanding and Using Rational Tools,* and to provide feedback on their skill in using rational tools for quality improvement.

Directions

1. Review this exercise as a team and ensure that your team understands what tasks it must complete.

2. Each team member takes fifteen minutes to review the descriptions of the following rational tools for quality improvement:

   • Flowcharting

   • Cause-and-Effect Diagrams

   • Pareto Charts

3. Review and discuss each of the tools as a team and ensure that each team member understands these tools.

4. Prepare for the facilitation practice rounds by having three team members volunteer to use one of the three rational tools for improving quality. Facilitator 'A' facilitates the first practice round, facilitator 'B' the next, and facilitator 'C' the final practice round.

Team Member	Letter	Tool
	A	Flowcharting
	B	Cause-and-Effect Diagrams
	C	Pareto Charts

5. Review as a team the *Observation Sheet*. Each team member will complete this sheet at the end of each practice round. There are three practice rounds and there are three copies of the *Observation Sheet.*

6. The designated facilitator sets the scene for practicing the rational tool. The facilitator may set his/her own scene or use of the scenarios provided.

7. Review the special instructions that follow and make sure the team knows how to proceed.

Special Instructions

Timer

Appoint a timer for each practice round. During each interaction the timer keeps time, limits each practice round to thirty minutes, followed by ten minutes of feedback and discussion.

Team Members

Team members undertake to use the rational tool being practiced and try to learn for themselves as much as they can about using the tool. At the end of each practice round each team member completes a copy of the *Observation Sheet*. These become the basis for the team's discussion following each practice round. All those who are not the designated facilitator are members of the team being facilitated.

Designated Facilitator

The designated facilitator practices using the assigned rational tool and facilitates the team's use of the tool. There will be three practice rounds in this exercise and three designated facilitators. Each will practice the use of one of the following rational tools:

- Flowcharting

- Cause-and-Effect Diagrams

- Pareto Charts

8. Follow the schedule below and complete the exercise.

    a. The designated facilitator sets the scene for the practice round (5 minutes).

    b. Conduct practice interaction (30 minutes).

    c. Discuss and give feedback (10 minutes).

    d. Repeat steps (a) to (c) for all three practice rounds.

9. Working as a team, identify any questions that you have about using any of the rational tools used in the exercise. Summarize your thoughts about when you might use the tool (Question 6 in the *Observation Sheet*).

Scenarios

SUITABLE FOR FLOWCHARTING

The team has been given the task of improving the current process for authorizing travel and issuing travel documents in the company. As a first step, the team is meeting to produce a flowchart of the process for authorizing travel and issuing travel documents. (Note: team members can provide input based on their current experience relative to travel documents in their own company).

SUITABLE FOR CAUSE-AND-EFFECT DIAGRAM

The team is a quality improvement team that is meeting to determine the reasons that teams don't develop a high level of commitment in team members to the goals and performance of the team. It has decided to produce a C&E diagram to identify causes and sub-causes for the problem .

SUITABLE FOR PARETO CHART

The team is a procurement team. It has met to identify and classify the major reasons that mistakes are made in procurement packages. In using this scenario, first develop a list of possible causes. Then use your collective imaginations and assign relative percentages to each cause which accounts for that cause's contribution to the total number of rejected packages.

<u>**HANDOUT**</u>   **Observation Sheet (Quality Improvement)**

This sheet is to be completed by all team members, including the designated facilitator, at the end of each practice round. After each team member has taken a few moments to complete the sheet, the team discusses its experience learning to use the rational tool.

1. How clearly did the designated facilitator present the purpose of the practice round, i.e., the setting and what the team was meeting to accomplish? If this step could have been improved, how might it have been improved?

2. How clearly did the designated facilitator set up the steps for using the rational tool? If this step could have been improved, how might it have been improved?

3. Did the team become confused at any time in using the rational tool? What was the confusion? How did it occur? How might it have been avoided?

4. Did the designated facilitator keep the team on track, i.e., following the steps in the rational tool in the correct sequence? If this step could have been improved, how might it have been improved?

5. What question do you have about the best way to use this tool?

6. Where, in your own experience with team meetings, might this tool be used?

Practicing Facilitation, Putting It All Together

Objectives

To provide participants the opportunity to practice the use of the six competencies in *The Model for Superior Facilitation*, and provide feedback on the full use of their facilitation skills.

Description

This exercise provides each participant an opportunity to practice all of their facilitation skills. Each team member takes a turn in the role of designated facilitator and facilitates the movement of the team toward completing a task. Each designated facilitator is observed and receives feedback.

Time

You must allow at least ten minutes for each participant to function as a facilitator, plus ten minutes for the feedback round that follows the last practice round. You must add time to set up the exercise, time for participants to shift roles at the end of one practice round and the beginning of a new round, and time for the evaluation round. If you have teams of six members you should allow two hours and forty-five minutes for this exercise. In the program designs in this sourcebook, we have limited the number of practice rounds to two and allocated one hour for the exercise.

Resources

Provide copies of the following for each participant:

- *Practicing Facilitation, Putting It All Together* (p. 211)

- *Observation Sheet (Putting It All Together)* (p. 214)

Presentation

1. Review the exercise and its objectives.

2. Assign breakout rooms, if used, and assign time to complete the exercise and return to general session.

3. Put the overhead of *The Model for Superior Facilitation* (p. 276) on the screen. Tell participants that they will now have the chance to practice all of the skills for superior facilitation.

4. Go over the *Observation Sheet* that participants will use for this exercise so that they are clear about the specific feedback that they are to give to each other.

Debrief

Each team will bring back three key learning points from the exercise. Review and discuss each team's key learning points.

HANDOUT

Practicing Facilitation, Putting It All Together

You have _____ minutes for this exercise.

Objectives

To provide participants the opportunity to practice the use of the six competencies in *The Model for Superior Facilitation*, and provide feedback on the full use of their facilitation skills.

Directions

1. Review this exercise as a team to ensure that your team understands what tasks it must complete.

2. Each team member will have the opportunity to practice the skills for superior facilitation and facilitate a brief team meeting.

3. The team firsts selects a task that it will undertake. The suggestions below may be used. In this exercise each person on the team functions as a designated facilitator for ten minutes. The first facilitator begins the meeting. Then, another team member picks up when time is called on the first facilitator. Another team member picks up the process from the second facilitator, and so on until everyone has functioned as a facilitator. If the team tires of a task or feels that it has finished a task, before all members have served as the designated facilitator, then select a new task and continue the exercise.

   Possible team tasks:

   - Develop a plan that most companies could use to improve customer satisfaction.

   - Develop a plan for training managers to function in modern organizations.

   - Develop a plan that most companies could use to improve supplier *performance*.

   - Develop a plan for empowering people that most companies could use.

   - Develop a plan for total quality training that most companies could use.

4. Review the *Observation Sheet* and ensure that all team members understand what they are to record on the sheet when they are the observer/timer in the exercise.

5. Prepare for the practice facilitation session by assigning each member of your team (the people at your table) a letter.

Letter	Team Member
A	
B	
C	
D	
E	
F	
G	
H	

6. Review the information that follows and make sure the team knows how to proceed.

Special Instructions

Observer/Timer

Does the following:

- Runs the video (if used).

- Observes the *performance* of the designated facilitator during each interaction.

- Completes the *Observation Sheet* on the person serving as designated facilitator.

- At the end of the exercise, gives the completed Observation sheet to the person observed during the feedback rounds.

Designated Facilitator

Each team member will take a turn being the designated facilitator. As each facilitator completes a practice round, the next facilitator takes over, and so on until all members have served as a facilitator.

Team Member

Every person who is not the observer/timer or the designated facilitator serves as a team member and participates with other team members to complete the team's task.

Feedback Round

After all team members have served as a designated facilitator, members share the *results* of their observations with each facilitator observed.

7. Select a team topic.

8. Use the following practice schedule to conduct the practice facilitation rounds.

Time Sequence

a. <u>10</u> minutes for each practice round.

b. <u>10</u> minutes for feedback round at end of final practice round.

Designated Facilitator	Observer/Timer* and Team Members
A	B,C,D,E,F,G*
B	C,D,E,F,G,A*
C	D,E,F,G,A,B*
D	E,F,G,A,B,C*
E	F,G,A,B,C,D*
F	G,A,B,C,D,E*
G	A,B,C,D,E,F*

9. Conduct feedback round. Each person shares observations with team and gives the *Observation Sheet* to person observed.

10. Discuss the exercise as a team and identify three key learnings. Bring these to the general session for discussion.

<u>HANDOUT</u>   **Observation Sheet (Putting It All Together)**

Each observer/timer completes this *Observation Sheet* on the designated facilitator observed and uses this information during feedback round.

5 = Fully agree   1 = Do not agree at all.

Designated Facilitator:_____

Circle the number which represents your response to each item:	**Agree**				**Disagree**

The designated facilitator helped us:

1. Use everyone as a resource.	5	4	3	2	1
1. Use our time effectively.	5	4	3	2	1
1. Make good use of the information available to us.	5	4	3	2	1
1. Adhere to our team meeting norms.	5	4	3	2	1
1. Remain clear about our tasks.	5	4	3	2	1
1. Remain clear about our responsibilities.	5	4	3	2	1
1. Clarify the steps we would follow in performing our tasks.	5	4	3	2	1
1. Stay conscious of the processes that we were trying to use.	5	4	3	2	1
1. Get back on track when we became confused.	5	4	3	2	1
1. Keep our inputs relevant.	5	4	3	2	1
1. Keep our inputs concrete.	5	4	3	2	1
1. Communicate respectfully with each other.	5	4	3	2	1
1. Develop sufficient information on all topics discussed.	5	4	3	2	1
1. Explore alternatives fully before making decisions.	5	4	3	2	1
1. Encourage differences in opinion.	5	4	3	2	1

Comments:

_____

_____

_____

_____

Learning Transfer Tools

The materials in this section have been designed to ensure that participants do the following:

- Stay actively involved in their own learning process and assume responsibility for their learning.

- Organize their learning during the facilitation training programs.

- Reinforce their learning during the facilitation training programs.

- Continue to reinforce their learning after the programs.

- Apply what they learn in the programs to their jobs and in their work environments.

The transfer of learning is one of the more difficult problems that trainers and organizations face in the training and development programs they initiate and support. The short-term goal of facilitation training is that participants obtain new knowledge or skill. The intermediate goal is that they apply the new knowledge and skill to improve team meetings. The long-term goal is that, by improving team meetings, they improve the total *performance* of their organizations.

The materials in this section do not assess learning. The tools for assessing learning are such things as pre- and post-tests, anecdotes from participants, and feedback from the coworkers of participants. Using tools to assess learning can certainly be used in conjunction with tools to ensure the transfer of learning.

Types of Tools

Tools to transfer learning fall into two general categories:

- Tools which the individual can use without involvement with others.

- Tools that require individuals to work with others.

Whenever possible, both sorts of tools should be employed as supplements and reinforcements to each other.

When you plan your program, you will make copies of the materials from this chapter of the sourcebook that you require, e.g., if you use the *Review and Action Logs*, you must provide these for participants.

In what follows, you are first given a brief description of the learning transfer tool. After the tools have been introduced, the materials for each tool are provided in later sections.

Review and Action Log

The R & A Logs are a basic tool to help participants record what they learn and what they can do with their learning:

- How they can apply the learning.

- How they can reinforce the learning.

These may be used as:

- Individual learning tools.

- Sources for discussion and amplification by participants in their Review and Action Teams.

Be sure you have an ample supply of the R & A Logs on hand at your programs. We have included the use of the R & A Log in the one and two-day designs. If you space several one-hour or half-day programs over a period of time, you can use the R & A Log to help participants keep track of what they are learning in each session and to help them make the connection between one session and the next.

Review and Action Teams

Participants in a program may be assigned to a Review and Action Team (R & A Team). They meet at specified times with their team to review their experience in the program, their key learning points, and discuss their personal action plans. They use their R & A Logs in their review and planning sessions with their R & A Teams.

If participants are attending the program with people from their own organization, they are expected to meet on a periodic basis with their R & A Team to continue reinforcing their learning and to help members of the team continue to apply what they learn during the program.

If participants are not attending the program with people from their own organization, they will be expected to work with at least one other person in their own organization (a "buddy") to help them continue reinforcing their learning and continue to apply what they learn during the program.

Buddy System

When it is not possible for participants to meet with an R & A Team to follow up their experience in the program, it is recommended that they identify one other person with whom they may meet. If two persons are present from the same organization in the program, they are logical candidates.

Self-Mail

This method encourages participants to leave a self-addressed envelope with the trainer. Inside the envelope the participant records his/her improvement targets or a specific application that he/she intends to make—based on the program experience. The trainer commits to mailing the envelopes to each participant at a future date—two or three weeks hence.

Debriefings to Management

This method for reinforcing and transferring learning requires that participants in the program commit to arranging a meeting after the program with a manager in their home organization. During the meeting they describe the objectives and content of the program, what they learned from the program, and what they intend to do with what they have learned.

Notes

- _____
- _____
- _____
- _____
- _____
- _____
- _____
- _____
- _____
- _____
- _____
- _____
- _____
- _____
- _____
- _____
- _____
- _____
- _____
- _____

<u>HANDOUT</u>   **Review and Action Log**

Work by yourself and complete the *Review and Action Log* found below each time you are requested to do so by your facilitator. You will review your logs in your assigned Review and Action Team during the program.

Key Learning Points	How I Can Apply or Reinforce What I Have Learned

HANDOUT

Buddy System

One way for you to reinforce and transfer your experience in the program that you are attending is to identify a person with whom you will meet after the program for at least three sessions to discuss what you learned in the program and what you are doing to improve your facilitation training. Complete this planning sheet before you leave the program.

1. Name of person with whom I will meet:

_____

2. By what date will I have the first meeting?

_____

3. What specific topics do I want to discuss at the first meeting?

_____

_____

_____

_____

_____

_____

_____

_____

_____

_____

_____

<u>Handout</u>

Self-Mail

To help you reinforce and apply your experience in the facilitation training program that you are completing to your job and work environment, i.e., to do something concrete about what you have learned, you can send yourself a letter. The process is:

1. Complete this form.

2. Seal it in an envelope that your trainer will give you.

3. Address the envelope to yourself. Your trainer will mail the letter to you in two or three weeks.

Letter to myself:

I expect to apply what I have learned about superior facilitation in the following specific ways:

_____

_____

_____

I plan to learn more about the following:

_____

_____

_____

I plan to describe to the following people what I learned in the program:

_____

_____

_____

I plan to gain feedback about my facilitation skills in the following ways:

_____

_____

_____

HANDOUT

Debriefing to Management

To help you reinforce and transfer your experience in the program that you are completing to your job and work environment, i.e., to do something concrete about what you have learned, you are encouraged to plan and conduct a debriefing for a manager in your organization. To plan your debriefing, complete the following:

1. Name of the manager to be debriefed:

2. The date by which I intend to hold the debriefing:

3. The specific things that I learned in the facilitation training program:

4. How I might involve the manager in a mutual process to improve my facilitation skills:

Program Evaluation Forms

You will find two forms in this section for evaluating participants' reactions to your facilitation training programs. The short form is for evaluating the brief one-hour and half-day training programs. The long form is for evaluating the one-day, two-day, and three-day programs. It is clear that one-hour training programs cannot carry the burden of lengthy evaluation processes, unless, of course, you are evaluating a whole series of such programs that have been offered over a period of time.

HANDOUT   **Program Evaluation: Short Form**

Date: _____

Please complete this evaluation sheet before you leave the program and return it to the person designated by your facilitator.

5 = Totally Agree   1 = Totally Disagree.

Circle the number which represents your response to each item:	**Agree**				**Disagree**
1. I received sufficient information to permit me to plan properly to attend the program.	5	4	3	2	1
2. I was notified in sufficient time to permit me to plan properly to attend the program.	5	4	3	2	1
3. The training rooms were excellent.	5	4	3	2	1
4. The quality of the training materials was excellent.	5	4	3	2	1
5. The quality of instruction was excellent.	5	4	3	2	1
6. I believe my experience in the program has provided me with tools that can help me improve my performance.	5	4	3	2	1
7. I would recommend this program to others without reservation.	5	4	3	2	1

General Comments

Provide below any additional comments that you would like to make about the program that you have just attended:

_____

_____

_____

_____

_____

_____

_____

_____

_____

_____

_____

<u>**HANDOUT**</u>   **Program Evaluation: Long Form**

Date:_____

Please complete this evaluation sheet before you leave the program and return it to the person designated by your instructor.

5 = Totally Agree   1 = Totally Disagree.

Circle the number which represents your response to each item:	**Agree**				**Disagree**

Administration/Facilities

1. I received sufficient information to permit me to plan properly to attend the program.	5	4	3	2	1
2. I was notified in sufficient time to permit me to plan properly to attend the program.	5	4	3	2	1
3. The training rooms were excellent.	5	4	3	2	1
4. Support during the program was excellent.	5	4	3	2	1

Make comments here, if you like, about administration of program and facilities :

Program

5. The quality of the training materials was excellent.	5	4	3	2	1
6. The quality of instruction was excellent.	5	4	3	2	1
7. I believe my experience in the program has provided me with tools that can help me improve the performance of my teams.	5	4	3	2	1
8. I would recommend this program to others without reservation.	5	4	3	2	1

Make comments here, if you like, about the program :

Description of Overall Experience

9. Write below short phrases or adjectives which describe your overall experience in this program:

_____

_____

_____

_____

_____

_____

_____

_____

_____

_____

_____

_____

_____

_____

_____

_____

_____

_____

_____

_____

_____

_____

_____

_____

_____

_____

_____

_____

Chapter Nine:

Using the Assessment Tools

These are the assessment tools found in this chapter:

- Facilitation Analysis Questionnaire: *Self*

- Facilitation Analysis Questionnaire (FAQ): *Other*

- Facilitator Competencies Assessment (FCA)

- Follow-Up Interview

- Follow-Up Questionnaire

- Pre- and Post-Program Videotaping

USING THE ASSESSMENT TOOLS

You may use the assessment tools in two ways :

- Key them into your word processing system "as is" or customize them to suit your specific needs .
- Photocopy the tools that you need from this book and use them "as is."

TRAINER'S NOTES

Using Facilitation Analysis Questionnaire (FAQ)

The FAQ measures the self-perception that individuals have of the way they think they do or would approach the task of facilitation. The FAQ has two forms, *Self* and *Other*. The *Self* form can be used by itself, or it can be combined with the FAQ, *Other*, which is filled out on the participant by coworkers. When the *Other* form is used, it must be completed before the start of a training program. Data from coworkers should be anonymous and should be summarized by the trainer for each participant.

<u>**HANDOUT**</u>   **Facilitation Analysis Questionnaire (FAQ): Self**

Directions   Please fill in your name and the date and then follow the directions
                        below and complete the questionnaire.

                        Name: _____

                        Date: _____

                        To what degree do you believe that the following statements are
                        characteristic of your behaviors or performance? Circle the number
                        that you believe applies to you for each statement.

5	4	3	2	1
Very Characteristic	**Moderately Characteristic**	**Somewhat Characteristic**	**Moderately Uncharacteristic**	**Very Uncharacteristic**

When I work with others during a team meeting:

1. I help the team use all of the resources of its members.   5   4   3   2   1

2. I help the team use its time effectively.   5   4   3   2   1

3. I help the team make good use of the information it has available. 5   4   3   2   1

4. I help the team develop clear norms to follow during its meetings. 5   4   3   2   1

5. I help the team remain clear about its tasks.   5   4   3   2   1

6. I help the team clarify the steps it will follow in performing its tasks. 5   4   3   2   1

7. I help the team stay conscious of what it is doing.   5   4   3   2   1

8. I help the team get back on track when it becomes confused.   5   4   3   2   1

9. When I make inputs at a team meeting they are always relevant.   5   4   3   2   1

10. When I make inputs at a team meeting, they are always concrete. 1   2   3   4   5

11. When I make inputs at a team meeting, they are always respectful. 1   2   3   4   5

12. I always help the team develop sufficient information before it
    makes a decision.   1   2   3   4   5

13. I encourage team members to express differences of opinion.   1   2   3   4   5

14. I often help the team use a variety of problem solving tools,
    like brainstorming and Pareto charts.   1   2   3   4   5

<u>HANDOUT</u>

Facilitation Analysis Questionnaire (FAQ): Other

Directions

Please fill in the name of the person on whom you are completing this questionnaire and the date. Then follow the directions below to complete the questionnaire.

Name: _____

Date: _____

To what degree do you believe that the following statements are characteristic of your behaviors or performance? Circle the number that you believe applies for each statement.

5 Very Characteristic	4 Moderately Characteristic	3 Somewhat Characteristic	2 Moderately Uncharacteristic	1 Very Uncharacteristic

When He/She works with others during a team meeting :

1. He/she helps the team use all of the resources of its members.   5   4   3   2   1

2. He/she helps the team use its time effectively.   5   4   3   2   1

3. He/she helps the team make good use of the information it has available.   5   4   3   2   1

4. He/she helps the team develop clear norms to follow during its meetings.   5   4   3   2   1

5. He/she helps the team remain clear about its tasks.   5   4   3   2   1

6. He/she helps the team clarify the steps it will follow in performing its tasks.   5   4   3   2   1

7. He/she helps the team stay conscious of what it is doing.   5   4   3   2   1

8. He/she helps the team get back on track when it becomes confused.   5   4   3   2   1

9. When he/she makes inputs at a team meeting, they are always relevant.   5   4   3   2   1

10. When he/she makes inputs at a team meeting, they are always concrete.   1   2   3   4   5

11. When he/she makes inputs at a team meeting, they are always respectful.   1   2   3   4   5

12. He/she always helps the team develop sufficient information before it makes a decision.   1   2   3   4   5

13. He/she encourages team members to express differences of opinion.   1   2   3   4   5

14. He/she often helps the team use a variety of problem solving tools, like brainstorming and Pareto charts.   1   2   3   4   5

Using Facilitator Competencies Assessment (FCA)

The FCA is designed to help individuals assess and keep track of their competencies as superior facilitators. This tool is particularly useful as a self-assessment tool for individuals who regularly serve as designated facilitators. A person can complete the FCA at regular intervals and determine their level of confidence in performing the various tasks of a superior facilitator.

<u>HANDOUT</u>　　　　**Facilitator Competencies Assessment (FCA)**

Directions　　　　Beside each of the items listed below place a number that represents your own level of confidence in performing the task described.

1 **I have little or no skill doing this**	**2** **I have at least some skill doing this**	**3** **I have a good bit of skill doing this.**	**4** **I have a lot of skill doing this.**

_____　I can tell when a team has not structured correctly to perform its task .

_____　I know what to do to help a team structure itself correctly .

_____　I can tell when a team is not using the resources of its members .

_____　I know what to do to help a team use the resources of its members .

_____　I can tell when a team is not using quality communication .

_____　I know what to do to help a team use quality communication .

_____　I can tell when team members do not understand what is going on .

_____　I know what to do to help team members understand what is going on.

_____　I can tell when it would be useful for a team to use a specific rational problem-solving tool.

_____　I know how to use brainstorming .

_____　I can teach others to use brainstorming .

_____　I know how to use the nominal group technique .

_____　I can teach others to use the nominal group technique .

_____　I know how to use the gallery method .

1	2	3	4
I have little or no skill doing this	**I have at least some skill doing this**	**I have a good bit of skill doing this.**	**I have a lot of skill doing this.**

_____   I can teach others to use the gallery method .

_____   I know how to use consensus decision making .

_____   I can teach others to use consensus decision making .

_____   I know how to use the plus-and-minus technique .

_____   I can teach others to use the plus-and-minus technique .

_____   I know how to use priority analysis .

_____   I can teach others to use priority analysis .

_____   I know how to use flowcharting .

_____   I can teach others to use flowcharting .

_____   I know how to use cause-and-effect diagrams .

_____   I can teach others to use cause-and-effect diagrams .

_____   I know how to use Pareto Charts .

_____   I can teach others to use Pareto Charts .

_____   I can tell when a team needs to evaluate its performance .

_____   I can teach a team how to evaluate its performance .

_____   I can tell when conflict is developing in a team .

_____   I know how to mediate conflict in a team .

Using the Follow-Up Interview

Interviews may be conducted in person or by telephone. You will find below a list of questions that can help you make a judgment about:

- What participants learned from the program.

- What they have applied of what they learned.

Interviews should be conducted no sooner than two weeks after the program and no later than four weeks.

<u>H</u>ANDOUT

Administrative

Program content

Application of learning

Follow-Up Interview

(This information should be completed before the interview)

Person interviewed: _____ **Date:** _____

Date attended: _____ **Length of program:** _____

1. What information, ideas, skills, or other content do you remember that were covered or discussed in the facilitation program you attended?

2. (If the interviewee does not offer specific information about *The Model for Superior Facilitation*, then ask this question). Can you describe *The Model for Superior Facilitation* that was covered in the program? (If conducted in person, the interviewee might want to draw the model).

3. Can you recall any specific times that you have consciously tried to apply any of the ideas or skills that were covered in the program? (Help interviewee become as specific as possible.)

Using the Follow-Up Questionnaire

This questionnaire should be conducted one week after the program, but no later than two weeks. The questionnaire determines how much of the content of the program participants remember (they must have learned it to remember it). Indicate in your cover letter that the questionnaire is anonymous and that participants should answer the questionnaire without reference to any notes.

<u>HANDOUT</u>   **Follow-Up Questionnaire**

1. Describe or draw *The Model for Superior Facilitation.*

2. List the six competencies for superior facilitation.

a. _____

b. _____

c. _____

d. _____

e. _____

f. _____

3. Describe or draw *The Model for Successful Meetings.*

4. What are the four characteristics of quality communication?

a. _____

b. _____

c. _____

d. _____

Pre- and Post-Program Videotaping

In this method, a number of persons attending the program are matched with a same number of persons who did not attend the program. It is not necessary to use all the participants. If you use a random sample of twenty-five percent in a program of eighteen to twenty people, you can obtain a good indication of the results of the program.

Select any of the practice facilitation exercises in Chapter 8. Have persons who attended the facilitation program and those who did not serve as the designated facilitator in the exercise. Use the observation sheets *after* the taped interview is completed. Use at least three qualified observers to record the performance of the subjects on the observation sheets. By summarizing and averaging the information on the observation sheets, you can develop an evaluation of the performance of those attending and those not attending the program. The results from the two groups can be compared to demonstrate the degree of learning that took place in the program.

Chapter Ten:

Using the Rational Tools

Facilitators must be competent in using and teaching others to use a variety of rational tools to help teams perform such tasks as creating information and ideas, making decisions, solving problems, and improving performance. Chapter 8 contains exercises to help facilitators become skilled in using, at least, a few rational tools.

USING THE RATIONAL TOOLS

You may use the rational tools in two ways:

- Key them into your word processing system "as is" or customize them to suit your specific needs.
- Photocopy the tools that you need from this book and use them "as is."

It is beyond the scope of this sourcebook to try and identify *all* or even most of the rational tools that facilitators may use. The growth of total quality management movement and the many kinds of improvement teams that have accompanied the growth of the movement have placed more and more demanding requirements on facilitators to be competent in the use of more and more rational tools.

Introduction

What we have done in this chapter is to include a selection of rational tools that will have immediate utility for most facilitators in most situations. We have included tools in the following categories:

- Generating Information and Ideas
- Making Decisions and Evaluating Alternatives
- Quality Improvement Tools

Tools for Generating Information and Ideas

The tools for generating information and ideas that you will find described in this chapter are:

- *Brainstorming*
- *Nominal Group Technique*
- *Gallery Method*

Tools for Making Decisions and Evaluating Alternatives

The tools for making decisions and evaluating alternatives that you will find described in this chapter are:

- *Consensus Decision Making*
- *Plus-and-Minus Technique*
- *Priority Analysis*

Tools for Quality Improvement

The tools for quality improvement that you will find described in this chapter are:

- *Flowcharting*
- *Cause-and-Effect Diagrams*
- *Pareto Charts*

Tools for Generating Information and Ideas

This section contains the following rational tools:

- *Brainstorming*
- *Nominal Group Technique*
- *Gallery Method*

Brainstorming

Definition

A group technique for generating information that involves the spontaneous contribution of ideas from all group members. Requires the use of a flipchart or blackboard to display information generated by the team.

Procedure

The brainstorming technique employs the following steps:

1. Clarify ground rules for brainstorming.

2. Define topic or information target.

3. Go around to each member of the group initially and request ideas in sequence.

4. Record all ideas.

5. End with input in any order from members. Follow these rules in generating ideas:

    •   One idea at a time.

    •   Allow no criticism or discussion.

    •   Record all ideas, even if they seem repetitious.

    •   Piggyback on ideas.

6. Review all ideas and clarify—do not eliminate, only reword as needed.

7. Review all ideas and combine ideas that are redundant.

8. Review, clarify, and add to develop final list.

Nominal Group Technique

Definition

The *Nominal Group Technique* (NGT) is a highly-structured brainstorming approach to information generation and problem solving. It is a method that combines writing down ideas with brainstorming. The format of the method combines written recording with vocal discussion.

We have included NGT in this section with other tools for generating information and ideas. NGT, however, has a built-in weighted voting step that makes it a method that can be used for evaluating ideas and making decisions.

Procedure

NGT employs the following sequential steps:

1. A clear definition of the problem or objective of the session.
2. The independent and silent generation of ideas and information by group members.
3. A sequential and objective listing of ideas and information from group members.
4. A discussion and clarification of listed items.
5. Preliminary vote on item importance.
6. Final vote.

Step #1:   **Statement of Problem or Objective**

- NGT focuses the group on a specific problem, question, or objective. Examples might be:
  - What are the obstacles for improving productivity in our work group?
  - What can we do to increase most dramatically productivity in our team or organization?
  - Identify ways to measure the quality of our products.

Step #2:   **Individual Generation of Ideas**

The question or problem statement is displayed so the whole group has a clear view of it. Each member records his or her own responses to the question. Cards are typically used to record ideas—one idea to a card. Cards are taken up and used in Step #3.

Step #3:   **Recording and Displaying Ideas**

In the third NGT step, take up the cards with members' ideas and record the ideas on flipcharts.

Step #4:   **Discussion and Clarification**

All items are reviewed and obvious duplications are removed. Items are clarified. The potential usefulness of items is not discussed. Only duplicate items are removed from the list. Number items that have been charted for easy reference in later steps.

Step #5:   **Preliminary Voting**

Independent voting is used to avoid influences of status, personality and conformity pressures. Distribute an appropriate number of cards (at least three) to each member. Members review the list of ideas and select a number of items equivalent to the number of index cards they have been given. Members then:

1. In the upper left-hand corner of the card put the number of the item corresponding to its number on the posted charts (see the illustration below).

2. Review each item and select the one from their cards that is their first choice and place in the lower right-hand corner the number equivalent to the total number of cards. If eight cards are used, then the number for first choice is eight. If five cards are used, then the number for first choice is five, etc.

3. Select the card with the item that is least important or useful for the problem at hand. Place one in the lower right hand corner.

4. Continue to evaluate all remaining cards in this least-best pattern until all cards are used and the total number of permitted choices has been made.

Collect the cards and post the results. The preliminary vote is discussed to identify any strong disagreements and ensure that everyone has the same information and understanding.

Step #6:   **Final Vote**

A final vote is taken (if it is necessary to reduce the list further). The same procedure can be followed as that used in Step #5, or various weighting techniques can be used.

```
┌─────────────────────────────────────────┐
│  Chart                                   │
│  Number                                  │
│  Here                                    │
│                                          │
│                                          │
│                                          │
│                                          │
│                                          │
│                                          │
│                                          │
│                                 Rank     │
│                                 Number   │
│                                 Here     │
└─────────────────────────────────────────┘
```

Gallery Method

Definition

The gallery method is a variation of brainstorming. It is a method that moves group members to browse among ideas (in the same way that a person might move from picture to picture in an art gallery). The purpose is to expose group members to each other's ideas and generate more ideas in the process.

Procedure

The gallery method employs the following steps:

1. Pin or stick flipchart paper to the walls of the room. Multiple flipcharts or stands can, of course, be used. Each member is assigned his/her own flipchart or piece of flipchart paper.

2. In this step the group may be doing any of the following: (1) identifying possible causes of a problem, (2) selecting the best solution(s) to a problem, or (3) selecting a problem statement for which members want to identify possible causes or possible solutions. Put the goal or purpose of the exercise in a place that is easily visible to everyone in the group. For example: "Opportunities to improve the quality of our performance." or "How can we reduce waste?" or "What causes overtime?" or "What new product might we produce?" or "How can we expand our customer base?"

3. Next, the group discusses the problem (issue or opportunity) from Step #2. The goal here is to make certain that each member understands the statement and knows what sort of information the group is trying to generate.

4. Each member of the group, working silently and independently, writes down his/her ideas on the assigned flipchart. Assign no more than twenty minutes for this step.

5. After members have completed Step #4, members walk around and look at the flipcharts of the other members. If members have new ideas during this step, they put their new ideas on the chart that inspired the idea. Assign no more than fifteen minutes for this step.

6. Conduct a second round of browsing and writing down new ideas (this is a repeat of steps #5 and #6). You may conduct a third and fourth round, if it appears the group has the energy and a fund of ideas that have not been developed.

7. After the last rounds of browsing and adding ideas has been completed, the group selects the ideas that it wants to examine further. Start by having each member identify the one idea that he/she thinks is the most promising.

Tools for Making Decisions and Evaluating Alternatives

This section contains the following rational tools:

*   *Consensus Decision Making*

*   *Plus-and-Minus Technique*

*   *Priority Analysis*

Consensus Decision Making

Definition

A decision making process in which all team members have a chance to influence, accept, and support a decision. Because of the iterative process involved, consensus decision making is not only a way to make decisions, it is also a way that new information and new ideas are developed in the process of making the decision.

Procedure

The steps in consensus decision making are iterative, i.e., you can expect to go through them over and over until the group has tested consensus several times and is confident that it has reached consensus. The steps in consensus are:

1. Hold a full discussion of the subject about which a decision must be made.

2. Identify where there is agreement and disagreement. It is useful to place lists of areas of agreement and disagreement on a chart or blackboard so all members can see them.

3. Try to reconcile the different opinions using such techniques as:

   - Worse case scenario.

   - Pro and con list for each alternative.

   Have people with one point of view state what they think the other points of view are to test understanding.

   - Ask holdouts what it would take for them to accept the majority decision.

   - Collect more data and further clarify alternatives.

   The goal of consensus decision making is to reach a decision in which no one feels excluded—one in which everyone feels at least partially represented.

Plus-and-Minus Technique

Definition

This tool permits groups to examine the strengths and weaknesses of any choice they may be making. It forces a group to look systematically at the relative merits of alternative choices.

It can often be used as an initial way to pare down a list of alternatives and eliminate those that have little merit.

Procedure

The steps in the plus-and-minus technique are:

1. Review the decision that the group is making, e.g., how to change an office arrangement, where to place a new store, whom to select for some position, what projects to eliminate, and the like.

2. List the alternatives so that the entire group can see them.

3. For each alternative listed, develop three columns. The first column is headed "Criteria," the second column is headed "Advantage," and the third column is headed "Disadvantage."

4. Under criteria, the group lists all of the criteria that should be taken into account in selecting the best alternative.

5. Discuss each of the criteria for each alternative. By consensus determine if a criterion is a plus for the alternative or a minus. If it is not possible to tell, or if the criterion is not really a plus or minus for the alternative being discussed, then leave the plus and minus columns blank.

6. Once all alternatives have been evaluated, discuss the data and eliminate the alternatives that obviously do not compete with the rest.

7. Review the remaining alternatives. Try to develop additional discriminating criteria and repeat steps 5 and 6. If no additional criteria are developed, then review the list of criteria and assign numerical weights to each criterion as follows:

   3 = of critical importance

   2 = of great importance

   1 = of moderate importance

8. Compute the weighted value of each alternative as follows. When a criterion is plus for an alternative assign the positive value of the weight assigned. When the criterion is a minus assign the negative value of the weight assigned. In this fashion, proceed through all the criteria for an alternative. Add the plus and minus weights algebraically for each alternative. Those alternatives with the highest positive weights are the best choices.

Example of Plus-and-Minus Technique

In this example, the group is deciding among alternative providers to deliver team development training for the various work groups and teams within the organization. It is making its decision from three alternative providers.

Provider A

Criteria	Plus	Minus	
Cost	✔		
Experience		✔	
References			
Empirically Based		✔	
Evaluation of Results			
Clear Training Materials	✔		
Follow-On Resources		✔	
Work with Similar Firms	✔		

Provider B

Criteria	Plus	Minus	
Cost		✔	2
Experience	✔		3
References	✔		2
Empirically Based		✔	3
Evaluation of Results	✔		2
Clear Training Materials	✔		2
Follow-On Resources	✔		1
Work with Similar Firms	✔		1

Provider C

Criteria	Plus	Minus	
Cost	✔		2
Experience	✔		3
References	✔		2
Empirically Based	✔		3
Evaluation of Results			2
Clear Training Materials		✔	2
Follow-On Resources	✔		1
Work with Similar Firms		✔	1

Based on steps 1 to 6, the group was able to eliminate Provider A. It then completed steps 7 and 8, but developed no new criteria. The weights are shown in the fourth column. The weighted rating for Provider B is 6. The weighted rating for Provider C is 8 and is the indicated choice.

Priority Analysis

Definition

This tool is another way to help a group make decisions like selecting the problem or opportunity that it wants to work on, or selecting the strategy that it wants to pursue to solve a problem, or take advantage of some new opportunity. This tool requires the group to develop a list of selection criteria and then assign scales to each of the criteria.

Procedure

Priority analysis employs the following steps:

1. Review the *Priority Analysis Sheet* on the following page. The analysis criteria are typical, but arbitrary. The group can develop its own, modify what is shown, or use the criteria as is.

2. For each criterion a scale is used to show to what degree the criterion is met by the alternative listed in the first column.

3. List the alternatives under consideration. If the group is trying to decide what problem it wants to work on, these problems are listed. If the group is working on opportunities (new initiatives, quality improvements, new products) these are listed. If the group is already working on a problem or opportunity, then the possible strategies that it may use are listed in the left hand column.

4. Once the alternatives have been listed in the first column, each alternative is evaluated using the scale that is appropriate to each criterion. Each group member will require a copy of the *Priority Analysis Sheet*. After the example sheet you will find a blank copy that can be reproduced.

5. After the alternatives are rated, the ratings are summed, and the total for each alternative is entered in the last column. Alternatives with the lowest scores can be eliminated. A final decision can be made among the top one or two by discussion, or by repeating the process.

Priority Analysis Sheet (Suggested Criteria to Select Problem/Opportunity)

Alternatives (Problems, Opportunities, Strategies)	Criteria						
	Importance	**Resources**	**Return on Investment**	**Degree of Difficulty**	**Approval**	**Group Capability**	**Time to Undertake**
	5- Critical 4- 3- 2- 1- Not Critical	5- Great 4- 3- 2- 1- Little	5- Great 4- 3- 2- 1- Little	5- Hard 4- 3- 2- 1- Easy	5- None 4- 3- 2- 1- Several Layers	5- Can Do Now 4- 3- 2- 1- Can't Do Now	5- A Few Weeks 4- 3- 2- 1- A Year

251

Priority Analysis Sheet (Blank)

Criteria

**Alternatives
(Problems, Opportunities,
Strategies)**

Alternatives (Problems, Opportunities, Strategies)										
5- 4- 3- 2- 1-		5- 4- 3- 2- 1-	5- 4- 3- 2- 1-	5- 4- 3- 2- 1-	5- 4- 3- 2- 1-	5- 4- 3- 2- 1-	5- 4- 3- 2- 1-			

Tools for Quality Improvement

This section contains the following rational tools:

- *Flowcharting*

- *Cause-and-Effect Diagram*

- *Pareto Charts*

Flowcharting

Description

The first step for improving a process is to understand it. Process flowcharting is a tool that contributes to an understanding of a process by making the process visible. Flowcharting has proven to be a useful tool because it:

- Provides tangible and concrete information about the actual steps in a process.

- Employs a process that is familiar to most people.

- Is easy to learn.

- Gets everyone responsible for a process involved.

- Helps further team formation and development.

Flowcharting breaks a repeatable work process down into its constituent elements and uses symbols to develop a visual display of these elements and their relationships.

Definition of Terms

Process
A work process is the movement or flow of some object through a sequence of steps from the point of some input to the point of some output. This flow typically includes the elements of transport, delay, operations, and inspection.

Object
An object is whatever moves through a flow and is acted on or changed in some way. An object may be a report, an idea, metal stock, car frame, plan, computer chip, invoice, or anything else that must be moved or modified in order to prepare it as an output to some other process or for delivery to an internal or external customer.

Transport
Transport refers to the movement of the object in the flow from one step to the next step. An example of transport in a manufacturing process might be the movement of stock for a crankshaft to a cutting lathe and then movement from the lathe to the next step or operation in the process. An example of transport in an administrative process might be the movement of a travel request from the desk of the clerk preparing it to a supervisor for signature. Transport also includes the communication of information or ideas from one person to another or from one operation to another.

Delay   Delay refers to the time that the object flowing through a process is waiting. Delay, for example, occurs when materials are delivered and await entering some manufacturing process. All materials in inventory represent delay.

Delay occurs in most administrative processes at points when decisions are required, additional information must be added to a report, and when signatures must be obtained.

Operations   Operations are the actions taken to transform an object from a less desirable to a more desirable state, e.g., a lathe operator changes rough stock into an axle, a welder transforms two plates in a ship's hull into a single plate, an accountant transforms tax data into a return, a drafter turns the specifications of engineers into finished drawings, a researcher transforms data into conclusions and predictions.

Choosing a Work Process

What we choose to consider a process at any given time is, to some degree, arbitrary. We may consider the entire set of steps in the flow of procurement, from request to the delivery of goods, as a single process. Or we may divide this large process into various sets of smaller processes. We may, for example, choose to treat the procurement flow as two processes that are joined together so that the output from the first process becomes the input for the second process. We may place the steps of initiating, preparing, approving, and forwarding a purchase request into the first process and put receiving, inspecting, and delivering into the second process. Or we might choose to break each of these two larger processes into the smaller processes of initiating, preparing, approving, forwarding, receiving, etc.

The limits or dimensions of a process are defined by some input and output. Wherever we can identify an input, we can consider that as the beginning point of a process. Wherever we can identify an output, we can consider that as the end point of a process.

Examples of work processes are:

- Preparing an order release.
- Preparing a budget.
- Conducting a safety inspection.
- Conducting maintenance.
- Conducting a test.
- Preparing an engineering design.
- Replacing an engine.

Uses of Flowcharting

Flowcharting typically produces immediate payoffs like:

*   Breaking a process down and making it easier to improve.

*   Highlighting duplication and non-value-added activities.

*   Providing the basis for developing metrics like control charts.

*   Serving to develop baselines for benchmarking.

Flowcharting can be used to help answer such questions as:

*   What is being done and why?

*   Where is it being done? Why?

*   When is it being done? Why?

*   Who is doing it? Why?

*   How is it being done? Why?

Procedure   The typical steps in flowcharting are:

1. Select a process.

2. Make a working draft of the process.

3. Give copies of draft to key people who have knowledge of the process.

4. Work as a team and develop consensus on how the process currently works.

5. Identify obvious opportunities to improve the process and make improvements.

6. Make new flowchart of revised process.

7. Select the appropriate control charts and begin to track the performance of the process.

8. Make improvements based on the statistical performance of the process.

```

# Flowcharting Symbols

Common symbols used in developing a flowchart are found in the diagram below.

### Flowcharting Symbols

○ Operation (Something is done)

↑ Transportation (Something is moved)

◗ Delay (Something is waiting)

▢ Inspection (Something is being checked for errors or faults)

◇ Decision (Point at which next step in process is determined)

### Example
(Metal Frabication)

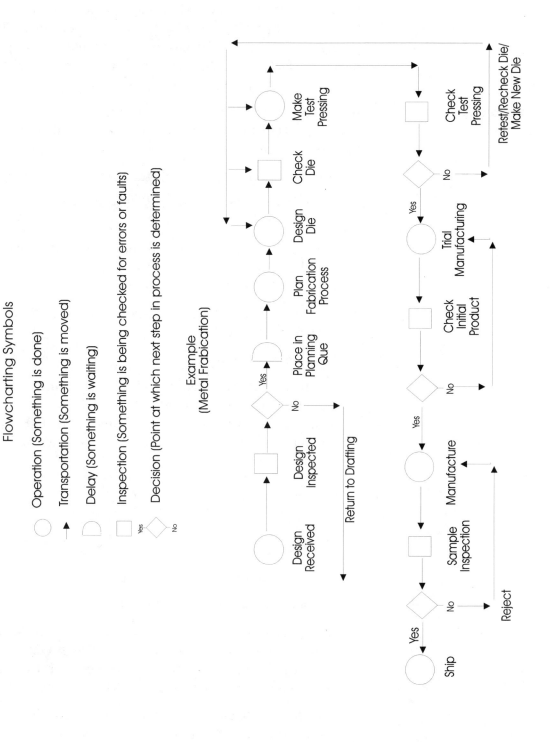

257
```

Cause-and-Effect Diagrams

Definition

CE diagrams have the advantage of displaying causal relationships. They may be used to identify the causes that create some problem in quality or performance. They may also be used to identify ways to go about improving or strengthening some desirable characteristic, e.g., greater sense of inclusion by team members or greater customer satisfaction. CE diagrams are also known as fishbone, Ishikawa, or "why?" diagrams.

Procedure

Information for the CE diagram may be collected by some structured process like brainstorming, the gallery method, or the nominal group technique.

The steps in developing a CE diagram are:

1. Put up several sheets of flipchart paper so that there is plenty of room to develop the diagram.

2. Select the quality characteristic or problem to be understood, e.g., delay, error, waste, failure, etc. The effect is something that we want to improve, control, or understand.

3. Write the effect on the right side of your chart. Draw a line from the left side to the "effect."

4. Develop possible list of causes by brainstorming.

5. Examine your list of causes and see if the causes can be organized into sets or factors. Above and below the line list the main factors which may be causing the effect. Often you will find that the main causes fall into the categories of:

   - Materials

   - Work methods

   - Tools

   - People

   - Environment (physical and cultural)

6. Connect the main factors to the effect line with oblique lines.

7. Onto each of the main branch items add the specific factors which may be causes as secondary branches. Onto these secondary branches add even more specific or discrete causes, and so on until all possible causes have been exhausted.

8. Eliminate those causes that don't fit the facts. Circle those causes which are the most likely ones that are generating the problem. The group may find that further investigation is required to verify the causes.

Example Cause-and-Effect Diagram

The illustration below is an example of a Cause-and-Effect diagram for analyzing the possible causes for poor stew.

Once primary causes have been identified, you may add second and third level causes. In the example of the stew, "mixed wrong," might be caused by no written recipe. "Dirty pot" might be caused by water temperature, and so forth.

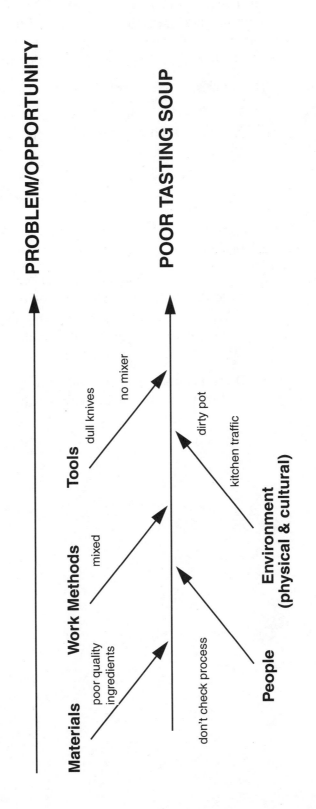

Pareto Charts

Description

A Pareto chart is a bar chart used to separate the "vital few" from the "trivial many." These charts are based on the general principle that twenty percent of the causes related to some performance problem account for eighty percent of the impact in terms of cost. The twenty percent are the vital few and the remaining causes are the trivial many. Pareto charts are useful for displaying attributed data in such a way that you can easily identify the cause or causes which are making the most contribution to a problem.

Procedure

The sequence for constructing a Pareto chart are:

1. Select the data that will be retrieved, e.g., kinds of accidents occurring, kinds of errors made, areas of customer dissatisfaction, etc.

2. Decide how data will be categorized or summarized, e.g., by location of error, by time of error, by worker, by machine, etc.

3. Design or select the tally sheet to be used.

4. Make observations and fill in tally sheet.

5. Make a bar graph by arranging categorized data in descending order of frequency. Divide the horizontal axis into the number of bars required for the number of categories used. Use vertical axis to measure number of observations in each category, i.e., bar.

6. Draw a cumulative curve showing how much each bar contributes to the total (100%) of all observations.

Example Pareto Chart

The following Pareto chart was made from data collected on errors in baking bread with a bread machine. It can be readily seen that the largest number of errors belong to Category A (liquid measurement error). If the first three categories of errors were eliminated the error rate would be reduced by over fifty percent.

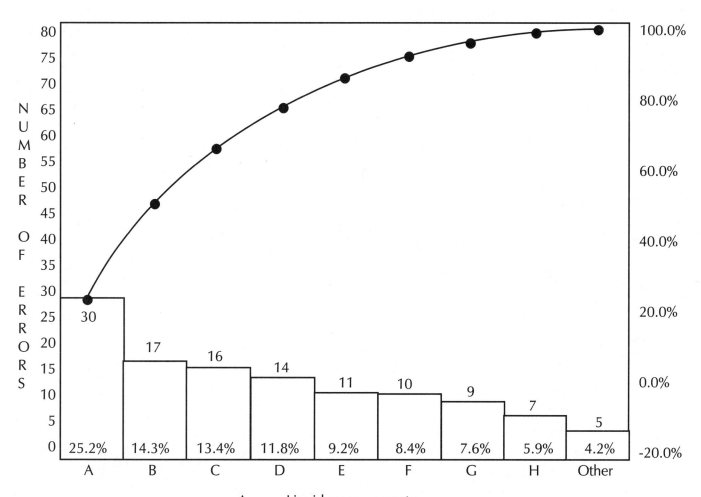

A = Liquid measurement error

B = Dry measurement error

C = Bad yeast

D = Omission of liquid ingredient

E = Failure to insert mixing rotor

F = Adding wrong ingredient

G = Using wrong settings

H = Omission of dry ingredient

I = All other causes

Chapter Eleven:

Visual Aids

This chapter contains overhead transparencies for all coaching workshops—ready to go "as is" or to be tailored to meet your needs.

USING THE OVERHEAD TRANSPARENCIES

You may use the overhead transparencies in four ways :

- Key them into your word processing system "as is" or customize them to suit your specific needs .

- Photocopy the overhead transparency masters that you need from this book and use them "as is."

- Photocopy the masters on plain paper and distribute them as handouts.

- Create flipcharts by handlettering the content on sheets of 2′ x 3′ chart paper.

Chapters 4 to 7 provide trainers with designs for one-hour, half-day, one-day, and two-day facilitation training programs. These chapters give trainers a sequence of activities for each program and identify the overheads or charts that trainers might use in conjunction with various activities, especially interactive presentations and reviews/previews.

In the next section you will find all the overheads or charts that are required to conduct the facilitation skills programs. Although these visual aids are called overheads, they can obviously be made into charts—either before a program or by trainers as they lead an interactive presentation or conduct a review/preview.

You will find it useful to make copies of your overheads and include these in the materials for participants. If you produce a participant's notebook, you will logically place overheads in the notebook in the order in which they are first referred to in the program.

Overhead Transparencies

The chapter includes the following overheads:

Introductory

- *Welcome to the Model for Superior Facilitation*

- *Welcome to the Model for Successful Meetings*

- *Objectives for One-Hour Program: The Model for Superior Facilitation*

- *Objectives for One-Hour Program: The Model for Successful Meetings*

- *Objectives for Half-Day Program: Introduction to Superior Facilitation*

- *Objectives for One-Day Program*

- *Objectives for Two-Day Program*

Program Flow

- *Half-Day Program Flow*

- *One-Day Program Flow*

- *Two-Day Program Flow*

- *Program Norms*

Models and Subelements

- *The Model for Superior Facilitation*

- *The Meaning of Superior Facilitation*

- *The Model for Successful Meetings*

- *Quality Communication*

- *Developing Understanding*

- *Special Functions of Facilitation*

Tools

- *Types of Rational Tools*

- *Tools for Generating Information and Ideas*

- *Tools for Making Decisions and Evaluating Alternatives*

- *Tools for Quality Improvement*

- *Review and Action Teams*

WELCOME TO THE MODEL FOR SUPERIOR FACILITATION

Your trainer is:

WELCOME TO THE MODEL FOR SUCCESSFUL MEETINGS

Your trainer is:

OBJECTIVES FOR ONE-HOUR PROGRAM:
THE MODEL FOR SUPERIOR FACILITATION

1. Familiarize participants with *The Model for Superior Facilitation.*

2. Ensure participants understand each of the elements in the model.

3. Ensure participants understand how the elements of the model are related to each other.

OBJECTIVES FOR ONE-HOUR PROGRAM:

THE MODEL FOR SUCCESSFUL MEETINGS

1. Help participants understand *The Model For Successful Meetings.*

2. Help participants understand how the model is a tool for superior facilitation.

OBJECTIVES FOR HALF-DAY PROGRAM:

INTRODUCTION TO SUPERIOR FACILITATION

1. Help participants understand the meaning of superior facilitation.

2. Introduce *The Model for Superior Facilitation.*

3. Introduce *The Model for Successful Meetings.*

4. Clarify the subelements in the model for successful meetings.

Objectives for One-Day Program

1. Assist participants in understanding *The Model for Superior Facilitation*.

2. Familiarize participants with the six competencies of superior facilitation.

3. Give participants the opportunity to practice facilitation and receive feedback.

OBJECTIVES FOR TWO-DAY PROGRAM

1. Assist participants in understanding *The Model for Superior Facilitation*.

2. Familiarize participants with the six competencies of superior facilitation.

3. Give participants the opportunity to practice facilitation and receive feedback.

4. Provide participants the opportunity to plan how they will continue to reinforce their learning after the program.

HALF-DAY PROGRAM FLOW

- *The Model for Superior Facilitation*
- *The Meaning of Superior Facilitation*
- *Understanding and Using the Model for Successful Meetings*

ONE-DAY PROGRAM FLOW

- **The Model for Superior Facilitation**
- **The Competencies for Superior Facilitation**
- **Facilitation Practice**
- **Lunch**
- **The Competencies for Superior Facilitation (continued)**
- **Facilitation Practice**
- **Review and Action Logs**
- **Program Review and Wrap-Up**
- **Program Evaluation**

Two-Day Program Flow

- The Model for Superior Facilitation
- The Competencies for Superior Facilitation
- Facilitation Practice
- Lunch
- The Competencies for Superior Facilitation (continued)
- Facilitation Practice
- Review and Action Logs
- Program Review and Wrap-Up
- Program Evaluation

PROGRAM NORMS

- Be informal and interactive.
- Take each other's comments and questions seriously.
- Listen to understand.
- Avoid nitpicking.
- No sub-grouping.
- Be prompt.
- Have fun!

THE MODEL FOR SUPERIOR FACILITATION

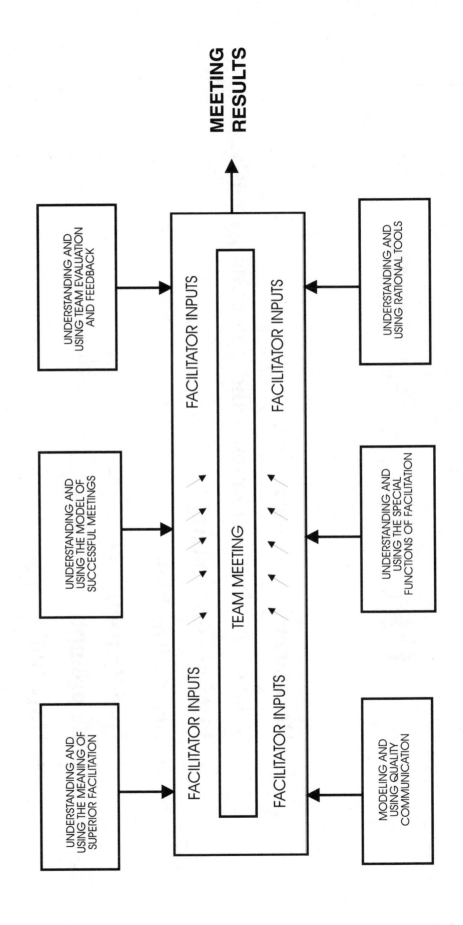

THE MEANING OF SUPERIOR FACILITATION

Superior facilitation consists of inputs (actions) by one or more persons that help groups achieve their goals and maintain or improve their competencies to achieve their goals.

THE MODEL FOR SUCCESSFUL MEETINGS

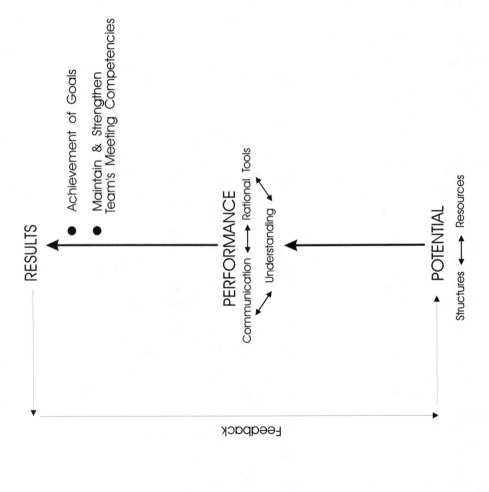

RESULTS

- Achievement of Goals
- Maintain & Strengthen Team's Meeting Competencies

PERFORMANCE

Communication ←→ Rational Tools

Understanding

POTENTIAL

Structures ←→ Resources

Feedback

QUALITY COMMUNICATION

- Interactive and Balanced

- Respectful

- Concrete

- Relevant

DEVELOPING UNDERSTANDING

- Inputs That Clarify
- Inputs That Summarize
- Inputs That Make Connections

SPECIAL FUNCTIONS OF FACILITATION

- Resource
- Teacher
- Mediator
- Challenger

TYPES OF RATIONAL TOOLS

- Generating information and ideas

- Making decisions and evaluating alternatives

- Quality improvement

TOOLS FOR GENERATING INFORMATION AND IDEAS

- **Brainstorming**

- **Nominal Group Technique**

- **Gallery Method**

TOOLS FOR MAKING DECISIONS AND EVALUATING ALTERNATIVES

- **Consensus Decision Making**

- **Plus-and-Minus Technique**

- **Priority Analysis**

TOOLS FOR QUALITY IMPROVEMENT

- Flowcharting

- Cause-and-Effect Diagrams

- Pareto Charts

REVIEW AND ACTION TEAMS

- Meet as indicated by facilitator during the program.

- Share and reinforce learning.

- Raise questions that need answering.

- If possible, continue to meet after program.

Recommended Resources

Bradford, L. P. (1976). *Making Meetings Work*. San Diego: University Associates.

This book has never been out of print since its publication. It provides a systematic analysis of the reasons that meetings don't work and offers many practical suggestions for improving meetings. One of its most useful sections gives a number of alternative ways to evaluate meetings and how to give feedback to group members.

Bradford, L. P. (ed.) (1978). *Group Development*. San Diego: University Associates.

This classic in the field of group formation and process consists of a series of essays by leaders in the field of group dynamics. Provides a good introduction into the theory of group formation and behavior.

Dewar, D. L. (1980). *Quality Circle Member Manual*. Ned Bluff, CA: Quality Circle Institute.

A very useful and practical introduction to facilitation. Focuses on teams which have been formed for the specific purpose of improving some aspect of an organization's performance. A resource for many of the more common tools used by groups to analyze and solve problems.

Dunsing, R. J. *(1977). You and I Have Simply Got to Stop Meeting This Way.* New York: Amacom.

A light and easy to read description of what goes wrong in meetings and how to make things go right. Of particular use is an analysis of the differences that often exist in meetings that take place in various settings, e.g., governmental, educational, religious, and health care.

Hart, L. B. (1991). *Faultless Facilitation*. Amherst, Mass.: Human Resource Development Press.

This is an instructor's manual for delivering facilitation training. It has a companion workbook for participants. It provides designs for programs that range from one day to five days. It provides very detailed information about planning a facilitation program and includes descriptions of a wide range of rational tools for solving problems.

Johnson, Dora B. (1994). *Facilitating Work Teams: 20 Simulation Exercises*. Amherst, Mass.: Human Resource Development Press.

This book contains a series of simulations that can be integrated into most facilitation training programs, or they may be used as follow-up training activities in team facilitation. The simulations cover both early team development situations as well as problems that can occur at any time in the life of any team. The simulations focus largely on topics related to quality improvement.

Kinlaw, D. C. (1992). *Team Managed Facilitation*. San Diego: Pfeiffer & Company.

This book is a radical departure from most books about facilitators and facilitation. The author takes the position that every team member can be a facilitator and every team can assume responsibility for its own facilitation. The book gives an analysis of the major elements that account for successful team meetings and shows how anyone can strengthen these elements.

Glaser, R., & Glaser, G. (1985). *Group Facilitators Intervention Guidebook*. Second Edition. Byrn Mawr, PA: Organization Design and Development, Inc.

A good resource for developing and enhancing the skills of intervention. The book provides information for recognizing problems in a group's communication and the practical inputs that a facilitator can make to help the group resolve its problems.

Reese, F. (1991). *How To Lead Work Teams*. San Diego: Pfeiffer & Company.

This book takes the position that modern group leaders must be facilitators. The book provides a neat breakdown of the specific tasks that a facilitator/leader must perform and what skills are required to perform them.

Index

About the Author

Dennis C. Kinlaw, Ed. D., has served as organization and management education consultant to over fifty public and private organizations. Clients have included: The Aerospace Corporation, The Bell Atlantic Corporation, Lawrence Livermore National Laboratory, NASA Headquarters, NASA Kennedy Space Center, MCI, General Electric, EG&G, Quad/Graphics, United States Coast Guard, Zenger/Miller, The National Institute of Health, and the Health Care Finance Administration.

He has served as faculty or adjunct faculty for Virginia Commonwealth University, The American University, The George Washington University, and McCormick Theological Seminary.

Dr. Kinlaw is the only private management consultant to have received the Public Service Medal from NASA for consulting and training services.

In addition to some fifty articles, Dr. Kinlaw is the author of the following books:

Listening and Responding, Pfeiffer & Company, 1981

Coaching for Commitment, Pfeiffer & Company, 1989

Trainer's Package, Coaching for Commitment, Pfeiffer & Company, 1990

Developing Superior Work Teams, Lexington Books, 1991

Continuous Improvement and Measurement for Total Quality, Business One Irwin, 1992

Team Managed Facilitation, Pfeiffer and Company, 1993

Measurement Planning Handbook, NASA, 1993

Measurement Planning Workbook, NASA, 1993

The Practice of Empowerment, Gower, 1995

Trainer's Package: Superior Team Development Workshop, HRD Press, 1995

"KNOWLEDGE AND HUMAN POWER ARE SYNONYMOUS"

*K*nowledge generates human performance. It doesn't take a famous quote or the picture of a tree to know that. But full potential requires the proper elements. Your professional growth can thrive, as a member of the American Society for Training and Development.

As an ASTD member you will get:

Information on the forefront of practice and technology

Access to colleagues around the world for idea-sharing

Opportunity to contribute to the advancement of your profession

through...international conferences and expositions...best practices...electronic resources and networking...benchmarking publications...personalized research assistance...and much more.

Join ASTD now... and become part of a worldwide association of nearly 58,000 leaders in the field of workplace learning and performance.

Call 703.683.8100. Or fax 703.683.1523
Mention Priority Code: MH5A
TDD: 703.683.4323

 ASTD
AMERICAN SOCIETY
FOR TRAINING AND
DEVELOPMENT

Delivering Performance in a Changing World